Canadian Special Public

Invertebrate and Marine Plant Fishery Resources of British Columbia

Edited by

G. S. Jamieson and K. Francis

Department of Fisheries and Oceans
Fisheries Research Branch
Pacific Biological Station
Nanaimo, British Columbia V9R 5K6

DEPARTMENT OF FISHERIES AND OCEANS
Ottawa 1986

Published by   Publié par

 Fisheries   Pêches
and Oceans   et Océans

Information and   Direction de l'information
Publications Branch   et des publications

Ottawa K1A 0E6

Canada: $6.00   Cat. No. Fs 41-31/91E
Other countries: $7.20   ISBN 0-660-12122-0
     ISSN 0706-6481

Price subject to change without notice

Disponible en français

Director: Johanna M. Reinhart, M.Sc.
Editorial and Publishing Services: G. J. Neville
Typesetter: K.G. Campbell Corporation, Ottawa, Ont.
Printer: K.G. Campbell Corporation, Ottawa, Ont.
Cover Design: André, Gordon and Laundreth Inc., Ottawa, Ont.

Correct citation for this publication:

JAMIESON, G. S., AND K. FRANCIS [ed.]. 1986. Invertebrate and marine plant fish
resources of British Columbia. Can. Spec. Publ. Fish. Aquat. Sci. 91: 8

CONTENTS

Address of authors: Department of Fisheries and Oceans, Fisheries Research Branch, Pacific Biological Station, Nanaimo, B.C. V9R 5K6. *Marine Resources Section, Fisheries Branch, Ministry of Environment, Victoria, B.C. V8V 1X5.

ABSTRACT

JAMIESON, G. S., AND K. FRANCIS [ED.]. 1986. Invertebrate and marine
plant fishery resources of British Columbia. Can. Spec.
Publ. Fish. Aquat. Sci. 91: 89 p.

Invertebrates are an important fishery resource in British Columbia, with over 25 species being commercially exploited. This report describes the biology and fisheries for all invertebrate species
fished, including crabs, shrimp, intertidal clams, geoducks, oysters,
abalone, and other more minor species. For each species, life history,
method of fishing, and characteristics of the fishery are discussed.
There is a general discussion of the problem of paralytic shellfish
poisoning (PSP), and resource management and future fishery pros-
pects are briefly considered.

RÉSUMÉ

JAMIESON, G. S., AND K. FRANCIS [ED.]. 1986. Invertebrate and marine
plant fishery resources of British Columbia. Can. Spec.
Publ. Fish. Aquat. Sci. 91: 89 p.

Les invertébrés constituent une ressource halieutique importante
en Colombie-Britannique, où plus de 25 espèces font l'objet d'une
exploitation commerciale. Le rapport décrit la biologie et l'exploitation de toutes ces espèces, notamment les crabes, les crevettes, les
panopes, les autres bivalves fouisseurs, les huîtres, les ormeaux et
d'autres espèces moins importantes. Pour chacune, les auteurs
présentent le cycle biologique, la méthode de pêche et les caracté-
ristiques de l'exploitation. Le rapport présente aussi de façon géné-
rale le problème de l'intoxication paralysante par les mollusques, les
questions de gestion des ressources et les perspectives d'exploitation.

INTRODUCTION

Invertebrates are recognized as an important fishery resource in British Columbia because of their considerable demand as valuable food products and their extensive exploitation by commercial and sports fishermen (Appendix 1). In British Columbia, commercial invertebrate species rank behind salmon, herring and some groundfish species in total landed value (Appendix 2), but they nonetheless constitute an important element of regional fisheries due to the significant number of individuals actively harvesting them. There are more than 2500 commercial fishermen harvesting clams alone.

This report discusses the biology of major invertebrate and marine plant species exploited on a commercial scale in British Columbia. Factors affecting their exploitation, including paralytic shellfish poisoning and management techniques, are examined to improve public awareness of the status of regional invertebrate resources. Many invertebrate species are successfully cultured elsewhere in the world, and mariculture research in British Columbia is considered a priority. Techniques to enhance yields in the face of more intensive harvesting are therefore also considered. For readers who would like to pursue certain topics further, a bibliography has been included. Locations of place names mentioned in the text are given in Fig. 1.

Background

The study and management of marine organisms is based upon biological characteristics of the species involved and the nature of the fisheries which exploit them. Species which have broadly similar life histories or which are exploited by methods with identifiable, common characteristics are often grouped together. Thus in British Columbia, fisheries researchers are organized into specific units studying;
1) fish which inhabit both fresh and salt water at different stages of their life cycle (salmonids);
2) fish which live near the ocean floor (groundfish such as sole, flounder, and cod);
3) fish which live in upper water layers (pelagic fish such as herring);
4) invertebrates which live primarily in, on, or attached to the sea floor (shellfish, such as clams, crabs, and scallops).
Also included in this latter unit are studies of invertebrates which may inhabit upper water layers (e.g. squid) and marine plants, which while not animals, are attached to the ocean floor. Within the Department of Fisheries and Oceans, Pacific Region, research on invertebrates and marine plants is the responsibility of the Shellfish Section of the Fisheries Research Branch.

1

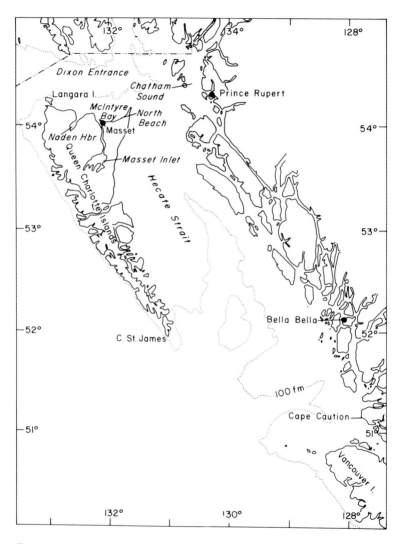

FIG. 1A. North Coast locations of place names in British Columbia mentioned in the text.

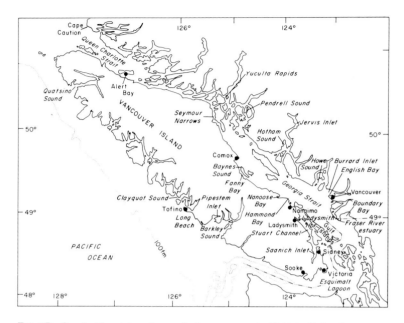

FIG. 1B. South Coast locations of place names in British Columbia mentioned in the text.

ECHINODERMS

Echinoderms, or spiny-skinned animals, are an exclusively marine group which begin life bilaterally symmetrical but which metamorphose into radially symmetrical forms. Common characteristics of this group include an endoskeleton of calcareous ossicles covered by an epidermis; a unique hydraulic system equipped with tube feet which are used for respiration, locomotion and sensory reception; the absence of a head and excretory organs; and a body which can be divided into five more or less equal parts, typified for example, by the five arms of a sea star or the five petals on the surface of a sand dollar.

Sea Cucumber

Sea cucumbers (Fig. 2), one of five classes of echinoderms or "spiny-skinned" animals, can be found from the intertidal zone to the greatest ocean depths. Approximately 1 100 species of these cigar-

3

FIG. 2. Sea cucumber, *Parasitichopus californicus*. (Copyright R. Harbo).

shaped animals, close relatives of sea urchins and sea stars, have been identified throughout the world.

The sea cucumber's body is relatively elastic in comparison with that of other echinoderms, and the skeleton has been reduced to minute, calcarious ossicles in the thick body wall. The mouth is located at, or near the anterior (front) end of the animal and is ringed by feeding tentacles which gather particles suspended in the water or deposited on the bottom. Almost all sea cucumbers are sluggish bottom-dwelling animals living on, or partially buried in the ocean floor. The largest sea cucumber found locally (*Parastichopus californicus*), is referred to as the California sea cucumber or "knob cod", and averages 25–45 cm in length. *Parastichopus* is found from extreme low tide level to 90 m depth. It occurs in locations protected from strong wave action and is most common on bedrock, although it also lives on gravel, sand, or mud.

Parastichopus is most often a light red to dark burgundy or mottled brown colour. The dorsal (uppermost side) is covered with stiff conical knobs and it lives with its ventral side in contact with the sea bottom. This latter side is paler in colour and bears numerous small tube-shaped projections called tube-feet, which are tipped with suckers and aid in locomotion. The sea cucumber's body wall is very flexible, mostly consisting of connective tissue and some muscle. Internal organs are simple. Sexes are separate with a gonad in the form of two tufts over the dorsal side of the gut, which has a single opening near the anterior end. Sea cucumbers have no brain, although there is a ring-shaped nerve chord around the mouth and a diffuse nerve system throughout the body wall. It is thought that their tentacles might be touch-sensitive for use in the selection of organically rich sediments and that their entire skin surface may be both light- and touch-sensitive.

Parastichopus is a sluggish animal which browses slowly over the bottom using its feeding tentacles to pick up and place deposited material into its mouth. The sea cucumber eats the microorganisms associated with the sediment particles it swallows and then, like an earthworm, passes out in mucous covered strings all the indigestible material, including sand grains and shell fragments.

Parastichopus breeds during the early summer months by shedding sperm or eggs into the water, where fertilization occurs. During this shedding, sea cucumbers adopt a "cobra-like" posture with the front end elevated off the bottom. The fertilized eggs develop into larvae which spend 7−13 weeks as plankton suspended in the water before settling on the bottom, where they change into miniature sea cucumbers. Small sea cucumbers are hard to find as many hide among marine plants, including kelp "holdfasts", and in rock crevices. Local populations seen by divers usually consist of similar-sized adults, suggesting that recruitment to adulthood might be low. Growth is thought to be slow, although to date no one has yet managed to age *Parastichopus*. Body size cannot be used as an indicator of age because the animals contract strongly when handled. There is a ring of five internal ossicles or plates around the mouth which might yield growth rings for aging studies as these are the only hard parts in sea cucumbers large enough to work with.

In October−November, many *Parastichopus* stop feeding and can be found containing no internal organs. Until now it was thought that the sea cucumbers "eviscerated" or spontaneously spewed out their guts at this time. Recently, however, some researchers have suggested the possibility of "atrophy" or wasting away of the organs rather than evisceration. New internal organs are regenerated in 4−6 weeks. Why this gut-loss occurs is unknown; at the moment it is one of the mysteries surrounding these perplexing beasts.

Although adult *Parastichopus* have few known predators, the presence of the sunflower star *Pycnopodia* and the sun star *Solaster* elict a violent, arching back-and-forth escape response in sea cucumbers, which is the only time they move rapidly. Young *Parastichopus* are more vulnerable to predation than their older counterparts, which may explain their secretive behaviour.

In British Columbia, a limited fishery for *Parastichopus* has been carried out by divers since 1980 (Fig. 3). Until the biology of local stocks is more thoroughly understood, management of the fishery has been, and will continue to be preemptive. It is expected that information on essential factors for fishery management of the species, including reproduction, recruitment, growth and mortality data

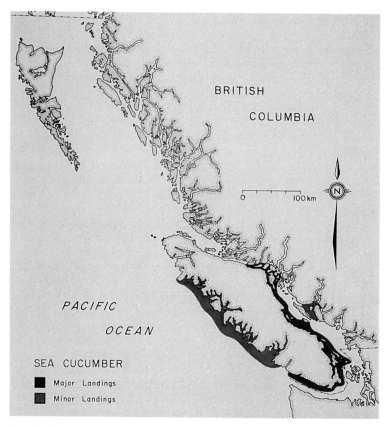

FIG. 3. The geographical distribution of the sea cucumber fishery in British Columbia in 1984.

should be published within a few years. At the moment, much of the coast is under closure although unrestricted harvesting is allowed in a few southern areas. Fishermen are required to submit a log record of their fishing activity, which provides researchers and managers with much needed scientific data on the abundance and distribution of the species.

Initially, there were only a few divers involved in this fishery, but by 1983, 43 vessels were reporting landings of 527 t. Densities of about $0.25-1$ animal m^{-2} (= per square metre) are needed for commercial harvesting. Diver harvest rates vary, but average about 2500 sea cucumbers per day (10 min^{-1}). Mean individual weight is approximately 0.65 kg, $12-15\%$ of which is marketable for human consumption.

In British Columbia, sea cucumber landings averaged 17 t from 1980–82, increased sharply to 527 t in 1983, and fell to 95 t in 1984 (Appendix, Fig. A). The landing in 1985 is expected to be about 350 t. In 1984, processors paid about $10-15$¢ per sea cucumber. Small sea cucumber fisheries have occurred in the San Juan Islands, Washington, since 1971, and landings there have averaged approximately 110 t since 1980. *P. californicus* and *P. parvimensis* are fished in Santa Barbara Channel in California. Landings in this fishery averaged 60 t in 1982 and 1983.

Although export markets have not been well developed for *P. californicus*, there is a domestic market for human consumption for muscle strips from the inside surface of the body wall (Fig. 4), and for whole, fresh body walls which are used as bait for fish. The main product of sea cucumber fisheries around the world are gutted, dried body walls, called "trepang" or "beche-de-mer" which are used to make soup in East Asia. The Japanese, who pay about 6 kg^{-1} for raw sea cucumber, eat the marinated body wall. It is particularly popular with hot sake on cold winter days. Also in demand are special delicacies such as dried sea cucumber gonads (approximately 100 kg^{-1}) and salted, fermented intestines (about 60 kg^{-1}). *P. californicus* could yield all these products although its body wall is too thin to provide high quality trepang.

Currently, with the exception of the Asian community, few Canadians have tried sea cucumber. Those that have however, can attest to the delicious flavour of the muscle bands when quickly sauteed in butter or cooked in chowder. The animals are easily collected by recreational divers and, at the moment, there is no recreational catch limit in British Columbia.

FIG. 4. Location in the animal of the five muscle bands which are marketed from sea cucumbers.

Sea Urchins

Sea urchins have spherical bodies armed with long moveable spines. In British Columbia there are numerous species of sea urchin, three of which are considered edible: the red urchin (*Strongylocentrotus franciscanus*), the green sea urchin (*S. droebachiensis*) and the purple sea urchin (*S. purpuratus*). In this report, "sea urchin" will refer only to the red sea urchin (Fig. 5), which is the largest and the only species which has been commercially exploited in British Columbia. Individuals of this species can have spines greater than 5 cm in length, and their actual color can be bright red, reddish-purple or maroon.

Sea urchins are found in a wide range of rocky habitats on exposed and protected areas on the outer coast, in Georgia Strait and in tidal passes. They are not found in still, sheltered waters. The sea urchin's vertical range extends from extreme low tide to 100 m depth. At any location, sea urchins usually have a distinct upper limit of distribution. They are most abundant just below this point, and abundance decreases rapidly in deeper water.

Sea urchins are herbivores which eat both attached marine plants and drifting kelp fragments. Areas inhabited by high densities of sea

FIG. 5. Red sea urchin, *Stronglyocentrotus franciscanus*.

urchins can be devoid of algae, and some of the upper subtidal zone of the B.C. coast is characterized by "barrens" maintained by sea urchins. Where high densities of sea urchins have been removed, dense stands of kelp often quickly appear.

Sea urchin densities in the range of $5-10$ m^{-2} may support viable commercial exploitations. Densities may reach as high as 50 m^{-2}. Such densities are found in areas with high current, often just below the upper vertical limit of distribution.

The life cycle of sea urchins begins with mass spawning of eggs and sperm into the water, where the eggs are fertilized. This takes place from March through July. Larvae spend at least two months drifting and feeding as plankton, then they settle to the bottom and change to adult form and begin to feed on microscopic plants.

Although small sea urchins have many enemies, adults have few. Predators include the sunflower star (*Pycnopodia helianthoides*), octopus (*Octopus dofleini*) and sea otter (*Enhydra lutris*). Other causes of death are starvation in winter, epidemic disease, winter storms and freshwater flooding.

Annual settlement of juvenile sea urchins is irregular in quantity, and can vary greatly over short distances. In the marginal habitats of Georgia Strait, annual recruitment rates are less than 5% of total sea urchin abundance, but elsewhere rates as high as 50% have been observed.

9

Interactions between sea urchins, sea otters and kelp form an interesting ecological relationship. Before sea otters were hunted to extinction in British Columbia, they preyed heavily on sea urchins.

FIG. 6. Location in the animal of the five gonads (yellow tissue) which are marketed from sea urchins.

Sea urchins were thus much less abundant than now, and kelp was much more widespread. Kelp beds provide shelter to small fish and produce huge quantities of food for local animals. The removal of the sea otter had a major ecological effect by allowing urchin populations to expand and limit the extent of kelp beds. Where sea otters have been re-established in Alaska, California and British Columbia, sub-tidal communities have quickly returned to their former state.

The gonads of both sexes (collectively referred to as "roe"), are eaten as a delicacy in many cultures. In particular, the Japanese pay very high prices for good quality roe, which they call "uni". Each sea urchin has five gonads located along the inside upper part of the shell, or "test" (Fig. 6). The gonads are used by sea urchins for food energy storage as well as for reproduction. The gonads become large when the animal is feeding well and shrink in size when food is scarce.

Colour and size are important factors in determining roe quality for marketing. Both depend on food supply. Gonads from well-fed animals are bright yellow, while poorly fed sea urchins have orange or dull yellow gonads. The gonads of starving animals are small and brown in colour. Dense sea urchin populations may yield poor quality roe because of intense competition for food.

The first commercial fishery for sea urchins was established at Tofino in 1970. However, this continued for only a few years before collapsing. Sporadic fisheries occurred over many parts of the coast throughout the 1970's. In recent years, fisheries (Appendix, Fig. A) have operated in Queen Charlotte, Johnstone and Georgia straits and on the west coast of Vancouver Island (Fig. 7). Sea urchins are collected by hand by divers. The fishery is most active from September to February, when the gonads are of high quality. Immediately after spawning, gonads have no market value, but they reach marketable quality again by early fall.

In 1980, a system of area quotas was implemented in Georgia Strait to prevent local over-harvesting. This caused the fishery to expand to Johnstone and Queen Charlotte Straits and the west coast of Vancouver Island. Although sea urchins are abundant on the north coasts of the province, most areas are too far from existing processing plants to permit a fishery.

Although the population size of sea urchins is not known, their widespread occurrence at high densities suggests a large stock. However, areas exploited in 1970–72 have shown as low recovery rate from fishing. Recovery in intensely fished areas was especially slow,

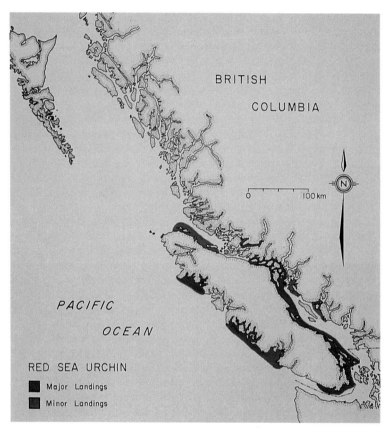

FIG. 7. The geographical distribution of the red sea urchin fishery in British Columbia in 1984.

and it seems such areas may take many years to recover. If sea urchins are to be managed on a sustainable yield basis, it is important to maintain a sufficiently high density of adults after fishing to ensure that juvenile survival does not suffer. Adults can enhance juvenile survival by sheltering the smaller ones under their spines. Sea urchins mature at a shell diameter of about 50 mm, and there is a minimum size limit in the commercial fishery of 100 mm to conserve a portion of the adult population.

MOLLUSCS

Molluscs (bivalves, snails, squid, and octopus) are one of the most abundant animal groups, encompassing an estimated 80 000 species. Common characteristics of this group include a lack of body segmentation; a definite head with special sensory organs; specialization of the ventral side of the body wall to form a muscular foot which is generally used for locomotion; and extension of the dorsal body wall to form a pair of flaps called the mantle, which secretes a shell and encloses a mantle cavity, typically containing the gills.

This chapter is divided into three subject areas: bivalves and snails, paralytic shellfish poisoning, and octopus and squid. Paralytic shellfish poisoning is discussed here because it can be a major problem with marine filter-feeding species, notably bivalves.

Bivalves and Snails

Abalone

The northern abalone, *Haliotis kamtschatkana*, is the only abalone species found in British Columbia. Abalone is the only snail commercially exploited in quantity in British Columbia. The spiralling low, open shell has a huge aperture at the bottom, through which a large muscular foot protrudes. This foot is used both to hold the abalone onto the rock surface and for movement; it is edible.

Northern abalone (Fig. 8), henceforth referred to simply as abalone, range from northern Mexico to Alaska; in British Columbia it is widely distributed and supports a modest fishery (Appendix, Fig. B). Most abalone are found on the outer coast. They require a firm substrate, some water movement (either current or wave action) and high salinity water. In both British Columbia and Alaska, abalone extend well up into the intertidal zone, where they can be collected by shore pickers. The largest individuals and highest abundance are usually found in the upper subtidal zone, within 6 m of zero tide level. Individuals have been collected from anchors and other gear to depths of at least 100 m.

Abalone concentrations vary greatly in abundance. Their density does not seem related to food supply; in fact, abalone are least numerous where food is most abundant, and often very abundant where food is scarce.

FIG. 8. Two northern abalone, *Haliotis kamtschatkana*. (Copyright R. Harbo.)

Abalone are herbivores. The very young feed on diatoms and microscopic plants growing on the rock surface. Juvenile abalone feed on larger algae and the main food of adults is drifting kelp fragments. Consequently, abalone are often concentrated near kelp beds.

Abalone breeding involves mass spawning and fertilization of eggs in the water, and subsequent larval dispersion. Larvae are planktonic for about a week, and currents may carry them to other areas. Spawning takes place in the summer, apparently triggered by water conditions.

Newly settled abalone are most abundant in barren grounds caused by intensive grazing of sea urchins. As a cue for deciding where to settle, abalone larvae use a chemical produced by a plant common on such barren areas. Settlement usually occurs in water deeper than where adults are most abundant. As young abalone grow and begin feeding on fragments of kelp, they migrate upwards toward the supply of drift material.

Unfortunately, northern abalone cannot be aged by rings or marks on the shell. Growth and natural mortality rates therefore cannot be obtained from age data. Growth has been measured in tagging experiments, and has also been estimated by analysing the patterns of animal size frequencies in the population. Growth is slow, and it may take 6–10 years for an abalone to grow to legal size. Growth rate is directly influenced by the amount and kind of food available. Abalone grow more quickly, and to a larger size, in beds of bull kelp (*Nereocystis leutkeanana*) and giant kelp (*Macrocystis integrifolia*) than they do in other algal communities. In some habitats, where food is scarce and of poor quality, growth can be so slow that abalone never reach legal size. Fishermen call these stunted individuals "surf abalone".

While juvenile abalone have many predators, adults have few. The octopus (*Octopus dofleini*), sunflower star (*Pycnopodia helianthoides*), wolf eel (*Anarricthys ocellatus*), and where present, the sea otter (*Enhydra lutris*) are major enemies, although these predators concentrate on other prey. In the low intertidal zone, birds such as the oyster catcher (*Haematopus bachmani*) and terrestrial animals such as mink (*Mustela vison*) and river otters (*Lutra canadensis*) may be significant predators.

There were some early efforts to harvest abalone commercially. A cannery was established at Jedway in the Queen Charlotte Islands in the first decade of this century, using abalone gathered from the low intertidal zone. Later attempts used hard-hat diving to commercially collect abalone. However, most abalone were collected only for private use until SCUBA diving techniques became well developed.

In 1976 a few large vessels, carrying crews of three to five divers precipitated rapid expansion of the fishery. These boats had freezers and air compressors, and so could exploit remote, previously unfished beds. Most abalone were frozen whole and exported to Japan. Landings, which had previously been less than 70 t per year, reached 273 t in 1976. Fishery managers then temporarily closed the fishery in order to establish more conservative exploitation.

The size limit, which had been 67 mm across the shell, was changed to 100 mm along the animal's greatest length in the early 1980's. Commercial licenses were restricted to the 26 previous participants, and were non-transferable until 1982. Fishery managers closed several areas for a variety of reasons, and required licensees to submit fishing logs showing harvesting locations, dates, divers' names, times spent underwater and amount taken. This information is used to monitor annual catch and catch per unit effort for each area.

License limitation did not reduce fishing effort. Landings in 1977 reached 428 t, so in 1978 the fishing season was reduced to 3 months. Total fishing effort still remained high, and roughly the same quantity of abalone was landed in 3 months in 1979 as was taken in 1977 in more than twice the time. In each of these years, the landed value of abalone was over $2 million, making abalone the second most valuable invertebrate fishery in British Columbia after shrimp.

Since 1979, explicit quotas have been placed on the fishery and the minimum size limit has been 100 mm. Annual quotas for the years 1979–81 were 226.8, 113.4, and 90.7 t, respectively. These quotas were applied on a coastwide basis; except for closed areas, there was no restriction on landings from individual areas. However, half the 1979 quota, and all subsequent quotas were divided evenly among the license holders. This restriction reduced the incentive for fishing in remote areas, shifting the centre of effort away from the Queen Charlotte Islands toward the mainland coast (Fig. 9).

As changes in the nature of the fishery have occurred, management problems have also changed. Recreational pressure has increased, and remote areas have become more accessible to divers. The relative magnitude of poaching has also become a management concern. In recent years, populations have continued to decline and annual quotas have been reduced accordingly. The quota will be 47.2 t in 1986, and the estimated landed value will be about $500,000.

It was once thought that fisheries for abalone could be managed simply by enforcing a size limit large enough to allow individuals to spawn at least once before being caught. However, the experience of other major abalone fisheries has shown that this method alone does not work. A large portion of the spawning stock usually consists of old, large individuals. Thus a fishery can remove most of the breeding potential of a stock despite the size limit. This may result in greatly reduced recruitment. Recent recruitment of abalone in British Columbia has declined greatly but the causal factors are unknown.

Intensive culture of abalone may be a future possibility. Abalone seed is produced by hatcheries in Japan and California, and experimental hatcheries exist wherever there are fisheries. In Japan, hatchery-produced abalone seed are sold to fishermen's co-operatives, which plant them onto natural beds and harvest them after they have grown. Similar projects have been carried out experimentally in California, where abalone are also grown in cages suspended from oil-drilling platforms.

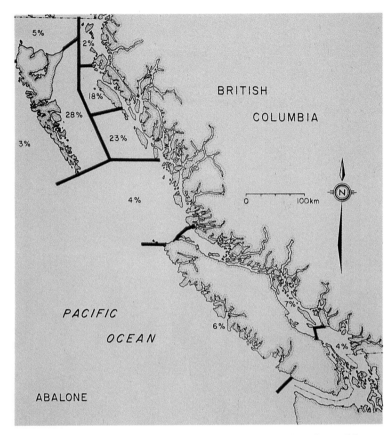

FIG. 9. The percent distribution of abalone landings taken from different regions of the coast in the period 1952–84.

The technology for spawning abalone, setting the larvae, feeding and handling the seed are well developed for Japanese and Californian species, but require some modification for northern abalone. Several possible projects can be foreseen; areas depleted by the commercial fishery could be restocked, private concerns could lease sections of the seabed to grow-out abalone seed, or hatcheries could hold abalone seed in their own systems until the abalone became large enough to sell.

17

FIG. 10. Geoduck clams, *Panope abrupta*.

Geoducks

The geoduck clam (*Panope abrupta*) is the largest bivalve mollusc in British Columbia, weighing up to 3 kg (Fig. 10). The name comes from a native Indian word meaning "to dig deep". Geoducks support both a small recreational fishery in the intertidal zone and a large subtidal commercial fishery which began in 1976 (Appendix, Fig. B).

Geoduck clams occur in a wide range of habitats in British Columbia. They are found from sheltered to moderately exposed situations, in substrates from fine mud through sand to gravel, and from brackish inlets to the outer coast. Their vertical range is from the lower intertidal zone to at least 120 m, but most populations in British Columbia have an upper limit near 8 m depth.

Counts of 40 geoducks per square metre (m^{-2}) may be obtained, but abundance is usually estimated to be $1-6$ m^{-2} in commercial beds.

Geoducks are filter feeders, pumping water through their siphons and removing plankton with their gills. Because geoduck siphons are up to 1 m long, these animals are found deeply buried in the substrate. Geoducks react to disturbance by withdrawing their siphons. Because food is least abundant in the winter, and because winter storms cause substrate movements, geoducks become inactive in the winter. They withdraw their siphons into the sand, and only highly experienced fishermen are able to find them.

Geoducks breed in summer by releasing eggs and sperm directly into the water. Normally all individuals in a population breed at once, with spawning triggered by water conditions. Fertilized eggs develop into larvae which drift as plankton for about 7 weeks, then settle to the bottom, change form, and assume a burrowing existence. For some months after the first settlement, geoducks are capable of leaving a particular habitat, drifting to a new one, and settling again. They do this by moving to the top of the sediment, spreading out a set of threads which act as a parachute, and letting water currents carry them to a new location. This ability is lost as the clam becomes older. In the first few years of life, young geoducks can dig vigorously in the sand with their specialized foot, and so can replace themselves if they are dug up. This ability is also lost as they become older.

Geoducks can be aged from growth rings in the shell. This enables biologists to estimate growth and mortality rates. Young geoducks grow quickly until they are about 10 years old, becoming old enough to be harvested around 5 years of age. Shell growth in length stops near age 10, but body weight continues to increase for many years.

The shell continues to grow in thickness, and very old geoducks have thick, heavy shells, often with irregular convolutions on the inside.

Geoducks may live to 140 years old, and have low adult mortality rates. They are sometimes captured by the short-spined sea star (*Pisaster brevispinus*), which can dig deeply into the sand. The sunflower star (*Pycnopodia helianthoides*) has also been observed eating geoducks, but only near short-spined sea stars. It is believed that the sunflower star steals geoducks from short-spined sea stars. However, these predators likely have only a small impact on geoduck populations, and biologists estimate the adult mortality rate to be less than 2% per year.

Juvenile geoducks are usually extremely scarce. This means that population turnover rate is very low; a finding which has a major bearing on the way the fishery is managed.

The effect of fishing on recruitment has not been studied thoroughly, but two opposing mechanisms seem to be involved. First, the fishery reduces the population of adults, which in theory should cause the rate of recruitment to the population to increase. Second, studies suggest that surviving juveniles are found mostly next to adults. From these results, one would expect heavy harvesting to reduce the sur-

FIG. 11. A commercial diver fishing for geoduck with a "stinger". (Copyright R. Harbo.)

vival of geoduck juveniles. Another effect is that fishing disturbs the habitat, exposing juvenile geoducks and other organisms. This attracts fish, crabs and sea stars, all of whom feast on the exposed prey. This may cause significant mortality of juvenile geoducks.

Hand diggers have taken geoducks from the intertidal zone on a recreational basis for years, often confusing geoducks with the smaller horse clam (*Tresus* spp.). Commercial diving for geoducks began in Washington State in 1970 and in British Columbia in 1976. A jet of water from a surface pump is directed by the diver through a nozzle (called a "stinger") into the substrate around the clam (Fig. 11).

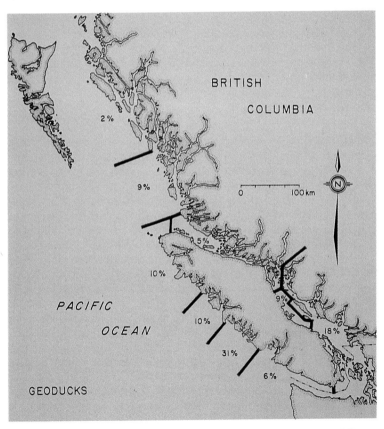

FIG. 12. The percent distribution of geoduck landings taken from different regions of the coast from 1976 to 1984.

Depending on the substrate type, the water loosens the mud or sand around the geoduck, or may be used to actually blow the substrate away. Divers prefer to work in water 13 m deep or less, but in the shallower areas where geoducks have become depleted the fishery is being forced into deeper water.

When the fishery began in British Columbia, it was concentrated in Georgia Strait and near Tofino. In 1981, the number of licenses was limited; in 1983, 53 vessels were eligible for geoduck licenses. When a system of area quotas was introduced, fishermen began to exploit the northwest coast of Vancouver Island, Queen Charlotte Strait, and the north and central coasts (Fig. 12). Some vessels are now permitted to partially process (shells and viscera are removed) geoduck clams at sea to improve product quality, and this is permitting harvesting in fishing locations previously considered to be too remote from processing facilities. Landings in 1984 were 3 483 t, with a landed value of $2.9 million.

Intertidal Clams

Over 400 species of bivalves are found along the coast of British Columbia, but only a few are utilized commercially or recreationally as food. Four species of intertidal clams comprise the major portion of landings in commercial and recreational fisheries: butter, *Saxidomus giganteus*; littleneck, *Protothaca staminea*; manila, *Tapes philipinarum*; and razor clams, *Siliqua patula* (Fig. 13). A few other species occasionally enter the commercial fishery and are utilized to a somewhat greater extent in the recreational fishery. They are included here, since greater use could be made of them in future, and include: two species of horse clams, *Tresus capax* and *T. nuttallii*; soft-shell clam, *Mya arenaria*; and the cockle *Clinocardium nuttallii* (Fig. 13).

Butter clams are one of the most common bivalves of the intertidal zone of British Columbia and are found throughout the coastal area. They are relatively large clams and can attain a shell length of 110 cm. The shells are white to grey in colour, solid and square to oval in shape. The species is found on beaches in a wide variety of substrate types, but its typical substrate is a porous mixture of sand, broken shell, mud and gravel. They are buried to depths of 25 cm in the bottom, inhabiting primarily the lower third of the intertidal zone, although they can occur to subtidal depths of 15 m. However, they have only been harvested in the intertidal zone. Growth rate varies

FIG. 13. Intertidal bivalves found in British Columbia. A. blue mussel, *Mytilus edulis*. B. sea mussel, *Mytilus californianus*. C. Pacific oyster, *Crassostrea gigas*. D. razor clam, *Siliqua patula*. E. butter clam, *Saxidomus giganteas*. F. littleneck clam, *Protothaca staminea*. G. manila clam, *Tapes philipinarum*. H. cockle, *Clinocardium nuttallii*.

from year to year, beach to beach and between different locations on the same beach, but is relatively slow throughout the province. The minimum legal size of 63 mm shell length for the commercial fishery is attained in 5−6 years in the Strait of Georgia, 7−8 years in the Alert Bay area and after 9 years in northern areas.

Littleneck and manila clams are frequently called steamer clams since they are generally steamed open, freeing the soft parts, which are then removed and often dipped in drawn butter before being eaten.

Littleneck clams are medium-sized, up to 65 mm in length, with solid oval to round shells. External surfaces of the valves have radiating ridges and colour may vary from white to chocolate brown; frequently they have geometric patterns. They are common, intertidal clams and are found throughout the coastal waters of British Columbia, frequently in association with butter clams. They usually occur on firm, gravel beaches at slightly higher intertidal levels than do butter clams, but range from slightly above the mid-intertidal region to the subtidal region, having been recorded as deep as 10 m.

Manila clams are similar in appearance and size to littleneck clams, but the valves are longer than high, giving them an oblong shape. The valves are heavy with radiating ribs, and their colour varies from greyish-white through yellow to buff brown, often with geometric patterns of black and white. The interior of the surface is smooth with deep purple at the posterior end. The tip of the siphon is split. These clams occur from about the 1 m intertidal zone to well above the mid-intertidal level on protected mud−gravel beaches. Subtidal populations are unknown in British Columbia.

Manila clams are native to Japan and were accidently introduced into British Columbia with imported Pacific oyster seed. Since the first discovery of the species in Ladysmith Harbour in 1936, manila clams have spread rapidly throughout the Strait of Georgia and along the west coast of Vancouver Island. They have not spread north of the Strait of Georgia through the Yuculta Rapids−Seymour Narrows area, presumably because of cold water conditions. Dispersal along the west coast of Vancouver Island probably resulted from plantings of oysters in Barkley Sound. In recent years, small isolated populations have been found in Queen Charlotte Strait and around Bella Bella; these populations presumably came from spawnings in the Quatsino Sound region.

Growth of littleneck and manila clams is variable. The minimum legal size of both species in the commercial fishery is 38 mm shell length. Both species can attain this size in about 3.5 years under optimum conditions in the southern part of the province and in 5−6 years in northern areas.

Razor clams are distinctive in appearance, with thin, brittle valves which are long, rather narrow, and up to 180 mm in length. The outer surface of the shell is covered with an olive green to dark brown shiny layer, called the periostracum. Although razor clams range from southern California to the Aleutian Islands, their distribution is patchy in British Columbia. They are abundant only in the Long Beach region on the west coast of Vancouver Island and on beaches east of Masset on the northeast coast of Graham Island in the Queen Charlotte Islands. The population in the Long Beach area is rather small and much of it is within the boundaries of Pacific Rim National Park, while the population at Masset is larger and has supported a small commercial fishery since 1924. Major recreational fisheries exist in Washington, Oregon, and California.

Razor clams inhabit surf-swept ocean beaches and have a prominent muscular foot that enables them to dig to depths of 0.6 m within a minute. They are found from the mid-intertidal beach region to subtidal depths of 20 m. On intertidal beaches, where harvesting occurs, clam density is greatest in the section of the beach closest to the low water line. Growth rate varies from beach to beach and between different locations on a particular beach; it is fastest at lower beach levels. On North Beach near Masset, razor clams in the lowest part of the intertidal beach attain the minimum legal size for the commercial fishery (90 mm) in about 3 years while at higher beach levels it takes 3.5−4 years.

Horse clams are common intertidal and subtidal clams in British Columbia coastal waters. Two large species, which can attain shell lengths of 200 mm, are *T. capax* and *T. nuttallii*. *Tresus capax* has nearly equilateral valves with centrally located umbones while *T. nuttallii* has valves that are elongated with an upswept posterior region with the umbones displaced at the anterior end. The shells are fairly thick but brittle. Habitats of the two species differ; *T. capax* is usually found with butter clams in mud−gravel−shell substrates whereas *T. nuttallii* is found in sandy substrates. Horse clams inhabit the lower third of the intertidal beach to subtidal depths of at least 3 m and burrow in the bottom to depths of 1 m. Growth of both species is fairly rapid; in the Strait of Georgia they attain a shell length of 100 mm in about 5 years, while in Queen Charlotte Strait they take about 6 years. Although horse clams are not harvested commercially to any significant degree, they are occasionally exploited by geoduck divers. In 1982, horse clam landings peaked at 321 t.

Another common bivalve is the cockle, which although widely distributed along the coast of British Columbia, is not particularly abundant in any one location. The valves are heavy with prominent radiating ridges that interlock at the edges and can be up to 120 mm in length. Large animals are light to dark brown in colour. Cockles inhabit soft, sand–mud substrates and are frequently found in beds of eel grass. Because their siphons are short, cockles are not buried deeply and large animals are often partly exposed. They have a large muscular foot, are quite active and can move across the beach. Growth is moderately rapid; animals of 60 mm shell length are about 3 years old.

Soft-shell clams are an exotic species introduced from the east coast of North America. They were first found in British Columbia around the turn of the century and since then have spread throughout the province. It is an important commercial species on the Atlantic coast, but has not gained much popularity on the Pacific coast. Valves may be up to 150 mm in length and are elliptical in shape, with a rounded anterior end and a pointed posterior end. The valves are unequal in length, soft and easily broken. The external surface is white or grey in colour with a thin periostracum at the ventral margin. Modest populations are found in estuaries. This species usually inhabits softer mud substrates at the mid-intertidal or high beach level.

Life histories of the species discussed here are similar to those of many other intertidal bivalves, including the Pacific oyster. Sexes are separate, with the exception of the cockle which is hermaphroditic, and sex can be distinguished only by examination of the gonad. Sexual maturity depends on size rather than age and varies with species. For example, butter clams are mature when about 40 mm in length, while littleneck and manila clams mature at about 20 mm. Time of spawning depends on species and environmental conditions such as temperature; in the Strait of Georgia horse clams (*T. capax*) spawn as early as late February, while littlenecks can spawn as late as October. Individual spawning periods may be brief, but spawning times for the population as a whole frequently extend over a longer time period. At spawning, eggs and sperm are emitted simultaneously into the water where fertilization takes place, with mass spawning of many individuals usually occurring to ensure fertilization. Vast numbers of eggs can be produced at spawning; for example, a single large butter clam can produce 50 million eggs in one season.

Larvae of the species discussed here are planktonic. The larval period varies with species and environmental factors such as temperature and food, but in the Strait of Georgia it is generally 3–4 weeks. Late larval stages are quite distinctive in shape as to species. At a size specific to individual species, they settle to the bottom, crawl on a well-developed foot until a suitable location is found and attach themselves to the substrate by means of byssus. After initial attachment they may break free and move about, either on the substrate or by drifting in the water column with currents. At about 5 mm shell length, they burrow into the bottom, remaining at that location for life.

Historically, clams were utilized as a source of food by native peoples on the west coast of Canada, as indicated by the large quantities of clam shell often bound in Indian middens. They were also important to early settlers and a clam fishery existed before the turn of the century. Today, the clam fishery is a relatively small component of the total landed value of fishery products in British Columbia, but it is widespread (Fig. 14) and does form an important part of the economy of some local communities along the coast. There are about 2500 commercial clam fishermen and as well, clams are widely harvested in the recreational fishery.

Fishing methods have not changed appreciably since white explorers first came to the coast. Equipment used is simple and inexpensive; some type of transportation to a clam beach, a lantern (since much commercial digging occurs in the fall and winter when low tides are at night), a fork, rake or shovel, and a basket. Diggers usually arrive at the clam beach 2−3 hours before low tide and work for a similar period after. The location of beaches with clam densities that will support commercial digging is largely a matter of local knowledge but an indication of clam density can frequently be obtained from the type of bottom, presence or absence of siphon holes or squirting clams, and test digging.

Digging methods vary with species being harvested. For instance, razor clams are dug individually with a short-handled, thin-bladed shovel called a "clam-gun". Diggers attempt to make clams produce "shows" on the surface of the sand by disturbing them — stomping on the beach or even driving a truck over the beach. A small wedge of sand is removed seaward of the show to expose the siphon which is then grasped quickly and the clam removed. If unsuccessful in the first attempt, commercial diggers usually move to another show since disturbed razor clams will burrow rapidly beyond reach.

Attempts have been made to develop mechanical harvesters to dig razor clams but they have not proven particularly successful. Problems have included mechanical difficulties when operating in surf, conflict with traditional hand-digging fishermen, habitat disruption and associated high clam mortality.

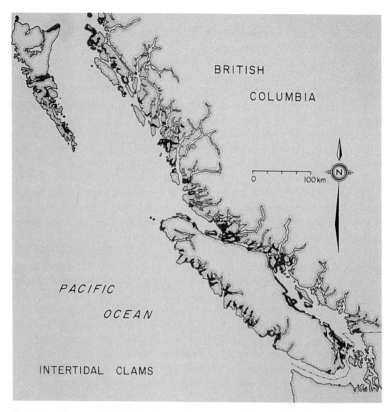

FIG. 14. The spatial distribution of commercial intertidal clam fisheries in British Columbia.

The traditional method for digging most other intertidal clams, particularly butter clams, utilizes an ordinary garden-type, long-handled, four-tined potato fork. Intertidal substrate is turned over and commercial size clams picked up, put in sacks and taken to buyers. Littleneck clams, which are frequently dug along with butter clams, are sorted out and sacked separately. On some beaches with extensive populations of littlenecks but few butter clams, diggers use long-tined rakes that are pulled through the soil to turn the clams out. Diggers usually use short-tined garden rakes to turn out manila clams which occur just below the surface of the sand.

28

Although a commercial clam fishery began just before the turn of the century, landings of individual species were not recorded until 1951 (Appendix, Fig. B). Consequently, only general statistics can be given for clam landings prior to this time. In 1984, landings for intertidal clams were 2622 t, representing a landed value of $2.8 million.

Fishery Characteristics

Razor clams — The commercial fishery for razor clams at Masset began in 1924 and has continued to the present. Landings have fluctuated from a high of 760 t to a low of 8 t, because of fluctuations in availability of diggers, markets, price, transportation cost and clam populations. The product was generally canned until the late 1960s, when the local cannery shut down. Since that time the catch has been used primarily for crab bait, and this has apparently resulted in reduced landings due to a limited market and low price.

Butter clams — Prior to 1950, butter clam landings ranged from about 450 t to 3 200 t. Since 1951, landings have fluctuated from 383 t to 790 t, with an average of about 600 t. These fluctuations were due to a variety of reasons, including influence by the state of the salmon fishery on number of active fishermen, availability of markets, price, the presence of PSP (paralytic shellfish poisoning), increasing sewage pollution which has caused closure of many commercial areas, and finally reduction in clam abundance on some beaches, particularly in the Strait of Georgia.

Commercial landings of butter clams have been made along the entire coast, but since 1963, the entire coast north of Cape Caution and much of the west coast of Vancouver Island have been closed to harvesting because of chronic PSP. However, the industry has adopted methods to process butter clams safely and some areas have since come back into production. Commercial harvesting in the north is only allowed by permit during the late fall and winter and is closely monitored. Prior to 1963, landings from the north and south of the province (north and south of Cape Caution, respectively) were about equal.

Littleneck and manila clams — Since 1971, strong markets and higher prices for littleneck and manila clams have focused the intertidal clam fishery on these two species. As with butter clams, landings of both littleneck and manila clams have fluctuated widely over time. Littleneck clam landings were at a low of 10 t in 1957 and since 1971, have ranged from 144 to 631 t.

After their discovery in 1936, manila clams spread rapidly in the Strait of Georgia and found quick acceptance in commercial and recreational fisheries. Manila clam landings followed a similar trend to those of littleneck and have ranged from a high of 184 t in 1952 to a low of 6 t in 1960 but since 1971, have increased and in 1984 were 1680 t.

Littlenecks occur in all coastal waters but virtually all landings come from the southern region. Littleneck and manila clams are marketed fresh and must be transported quickly, and this has proven difficult and costly for littlenecks from the northern areas. This may change because of recent strong demand and high prices. Until recently manila clams did not occur north of Cape Caution but populations are expanding in the central coast.

In addition to commercial landings, there is a substantial harvest of intertidal clams in the recreational fishery, particularly in the Strait of Georgia. However, there is presently no information on the extent of such exploitation.

Until 1966, there was both a seasonal restriction on harvesting butter, littleneck and manila clams, and a minimum size limit in both commercial and recreational fisheries: 63 mm shell length for butter clams and 38 mm for littleneck and manila clams. In the razor clam fishery, beaches were closed from June 15 to August 31, with a size limit of 90 mm.

The seasonal restriction has subsequently been removed for butter, littleneck, and manila clams. The size limit was retained for the commercial fishery but was replaced by a daily bag limit in the recreational fishery. Seasonal closure and size limit were both retained in the commercial razor clam fishery. Application of a minimum size limit ensures that clams become sexually mature and can spawn at least once or twice before they can be legally harvested.

Clam resources in British Columbia are limited and the question is frequently raised about the feasibility of increasing landings by farming clams. Clam culture is practiced in some parts of the world, and it would appear reasonable that techniques could be adapted to British Columbia conditions.

Experimental clam culture of manila, littleneck and butter clams has been attempted in the province, but difficulties have been encountered with obtaining sufficient quantities of seed (juveniles). To date, no natural areas have been located in British Columbia which could provide consistent quantities of seed. Consequently, seed for any farming operation has to be purchased from hatcheries, which is expensive. Hatchery-produced seed is usually small (2−5 mm shell length) and must be protected to prevent extensive loss, usually by some sort of netting. Loss is most often due to seed being physically washed out of the substrate and predation by crabs and small fish.

Limited farming of manila clams is currently being investigated by industry. With continuing research, improved technology, strong markets and high prices, clam farming may become viable in the future.

Mussels

Mussels (Fig. 13) are bivalve molluscs which attach themselves to various intertidal and subtidal substrates by secreting numerous protein threads which form the byssus. Although there are 11 species of mussels in British Columbia, only two are occasionally harvested: *Mytilus edulis*, the blue, or bay mussel (Fig. 15); and *M. californianus*, the California, or sea mussel. Not as abundant, but occasionally encountered, are two horse mussels, *Modiolus capax* and *M. rectus*.

Mytilus edulis is a circumpolar species widely distributed in the northern hemisphere. In the Pacific, it is found from the Arctic to southern California, and it has been introduced into Japan. A similar

FIG. 15. Blue mussels, *Mytilus edulis*. (Copyright R. Harbo.)

mussel is found in the southern hemisphere but it is not yet clear if it is the same species. In the Atlantic, it ranges from the Canadian Arctic and Greenland to North Carolina, and from the White Sea to north Africa. *M. californianus* is restricted to the Pacific coast of North America, from the Aleutian Islands to Mexico. *Modiolus capax* and *M. rectus* occur from Mexico to British Columbia.

Blue mussels, which can grow to about 80 mm, inhabit the intertidal zone to a depth of 45 m although they are most commonly found between the 1.5 and 3.7 m tide levels. They attach to rocks, gravel, shell, compact mud and many man-made materials. This species is tolerant to a wide range of temperatures and salinities and its distribution in British Columbia ranges from the heads of inlets to exposed coastlines.

Sea mussels grow to about 130 mm and inhabit exposed rocky beaches on the open coast. They most commonly live in the intertidal zone but have been found as deep as 45 m.

The two horse mussel species occur most commonly in subtidal waters but can be found from the intertidal to a depth of 50 m. They are found in crevasses and in mud bottoms, where only a small part of the valves are exposed. *Modiolus capax* grows to about 100 m while *M. rectus* can grow to about 120 m.

Sexes are separate in mussel species, although occasional hermaphrodites have been found. Reproduction is similar to that described for intertidal clams in the preceding section. When the larvae attain a length of approximately 350 micrometres they attach themselves to substrates. Settled larvae are called spat and until they are 1–1.5 mm long, may detach one or more times and drift, using their byssus as a parachute, to another site before settling in a permanent location. Sexual maturation can occur in the first year and spawning can take place in any season in the Strait of Georgia, although peak breeding occurs during the summer.

Growth rate tends to be extremely variable due to their settlement in a wide variety of habitats. Mussels inhabiting the high intertidal zone have slower growth than those living in the lower intertidal zone because they cannot feed when exposed to air at low tide. The greatest growth occurs when they are continuously submerged, such as in suspended culture. Time of year of spat set also affects growth rate, with those that set early in the spring having the advantage of being able to feed during the spring plankton bloom, whereas those that set later miss this bloom. During winter months when food availability is low and temperatures drop, growth slows considerably.

Mussels continuously suspended in water can grow to 50 mm in length in 12 months while intertidal mussels may take 2−3 years to attain this size.

Environmental factors, including wave action, abrasion by drift-wood, siltation and extremes in temperature and salinity, can cause mussel mortality. Natural enemies include predators (diving ducks, sea stars, crabs, sea urchins, snails, flatworms), competitors for food and space (barnacles, tube worms, algae, sea squirts and other bi-valves) and parasites (*Mytilicola orientalis* and pea crabs).

Other causes of natural mortality include fouling organisms, which add to the weight of mussels, thus allowing wave action to eventually pull them away from their byssal attachments; and poor settlement sites. Mussels that settle on sessile organisms can ultimately cause smothering and death of these organisms and their subsequent de-composition may result in mussel detachment.

Detached mussels fall to the lower intertidal or subtidal zones, thus increasing the chance of their falling prey to sea stars or being swept up on beaches to die from prolonged exposure to air.

The present mussel fishery is largely a gathering operation carried out at low tide using various scraping tools. These may consist of shovels, rakes, hoes or the gatherer's hands. Commercial landings in the fishery have been small and since 1975 have averaged only a few tonnes per annum. With the present scale of the fishery, regulation of the mussel resource is minimal. Harvesting is closed in polluted areas and in areas with paralytic shellfish poisoning.

The farming, or culture, of mussels has been successful in Europe for many years and more recently, in the Philipines, New Zealand and eastern North America. This success has led, over the past few years, to considerable local interest in mussel culture in British Col-umbia. *Mytilus edulis* grows quickly, has a high meat:total weight ratio and is nutritionally of high quality, making it a desirable species for farming.

Various farming methods used throughout the world include bot-tom culture, raft culture, post culture and longline culture. Raft culture and longline culture, using ropes and mesh stockings, were thought to be the most suitable methods for local waters. However, problems have been encountered because of extensive, unexplained mortality at some locations, mostly in late summer, and predation by birds. Methods of minimizing mortality are now being developed, a neces-sity before culture can realize its full potential.

In culture using mesh stockings, clusters of young seed mussels are gathered from intertidal beds or from collector ropes and are placed in the stockings, which are hung in the water from longlines or rafts. After a few days the mussels migrate through the mesh and attach to the outside where they have space to feed and grow. Re-stocking and thinning is necessary 2 or 3 times before market size (50 mm) is attained. The advantages of suspended culture include the avoidance of bottom-dwelling natural enemies, increased meat yield, a more visually attractive shell and meat, the avoidance of foreign matter such as mud and sand, and harvesting which can be carried out at any time, regardless of tide level. Disadvantages include high initial costs for suspension equipment, greater labour costs, and greater fouling.

Oysters

Oysters are one of the best known intertidal bivalves in British Columbia and are the only species of invertebrate presently farmed extensively in the province. The resource supports a valuable industry (1984: 2 897 t, $2.1 million) that is capable of considerable expansion. Oysters are also widely taken in the recreational fishery.

Three species of oysters occur in British Columbia: the native or Olympia oyster, *Ostrea lurida*; the eastern oyster, *Crassostrea virginica*; and the Pacific oyster, *Crassostrea gigas* (Fig. 13). All three species have been used in the commercial fishery.

Native oysters occur from Alaska to lower California and are found throughout British Columbia in modest abundance in widely scattered locations. They are a small oyster rarely exceeding 60 mm in shell length. The external shell surface is grey in color and seldom fluted. They are susceptible to temperature changes and consequently are usually found low on the intertidal beach on gravel or rock bottom, under rocks, or in tidal lagoons. Commercial landings of this species began in 1884 and continued until about 1936. The fishery was essentially for wild stock and in contrast to Washington state, they have not been cultured in British Columbia. Slow growth rate, small size and high labor costs preclude culture of this species under present conditions in British Columbia but it is exploited to a limited extent in the recreational fishery.

Eastern oysters were first introduced into British Columbia around the turn of the century. Transplants were made in the Strait of Georgia into Hammond Bay, Nanoose Bay, Ladysmith Harbour and Esquimalt Lagoon on Vancouver Island, and into Boundary Bay on the mainland near Vancouver. Eastern oysters can attain a shell length of up to 150 mm in length and are somewhat pear-shaped. The external shell surface is fairly smooth with concentric sculpture and a greyish to light brown colour. This species supports a large industry on the Atlantic coast of North America. It did not flourish on Vancouver Island but did reasonably well in Boundary Bay, where plantings continued until about 1940 and where a small residual population presently exists. Breeding has been limited and sporadic and *C. virginica* has not spread to other parts of the province.

Pacific oysters are the only species harvested commercially at present in British Columbia. They were first introduced into Ladysmith Harbour and Fanny Bay from Japan, in 1912 or 1913. They are a large oyster and may attain a length of 300 mm. Shell shape is irregular and is influenced greatly by environmental conditions. The external surface is grey in colour and highly fluted. Pacific oysters are common intertidal animals in the Strait of Georgia and in some of the inlets along the west coast of Vancouver Island.

The life history of the Pacific oyster is fairly typical of many of the bivalves along the coast. Sexes of Pacific oysters are separate, although sex reversal may occur from year to year. When water temperatures begin to warm in the spring, oysters convert stored glycogen into either eggs or sperm. In most British Columbia waters, oysters are fully ripe by early July. The sex of the oyster, as with most bivalves, can only be determined by examination of the reproductive tissue. The mechanism that triggers spawning is not completely understood but water temperature is important. A temperature of 20°C appears necessary to trigger wide-scale spawning.

At spawning, eggs and sperm are expelled into the water where fertilization takes place; the number of eggs that a single female can release at spawning may be as high as fifty million. Within about 48 hours the fertilized egg develops into a larva that has two valves. Larvae can swim weakly but are at the mercy of water currents. They can travel over considerable distances from the time of spawning until they are ready to settle.

Larvae feed on microscopic plants in the plankton. Growth depends on water temperature, but at 20°C they reach a shell length of about 300 micrometres in 3 weeks, and are then ready to settle. When they come in contact with a clean, hard surface, such as an oyster shell, they crawl around the surface on a well-developed foot and, when a suitable spot is found, secrete a tiny amount of cement from a gland in the foot and place the left valve in the cement. When it hardens, they remain there for life. This process is called setting or spatting and young oysters are called spat.

In native oysters, initial larval development occurs in the brood chamber of the adult, and larvae are released to the plankton at a larger size. Once in the plankton, development is similar to that of Pacific oysters.

After settlement, oysters feed on small plants in the plankton and lose some of their larval organs. Growth can be fairly rapid if water temperatures remain warm. Spat can attain a shell diameter of 25 mm by the fall and at this stage, they are referred to as "seed". Sexual maturity is a function of size rather than age and if growth is rapid they can mature during the following summer.

A prerequisite for any culture operation is a plentiful, reliable and inexpensive supply of seed. In British Columbia, Pacific oysters are at the northern periphery of their breeding range and there has been inconsistent natural breeding primarily because of low summer water temperatures. A major breeding occurred in Ladysmith Harbour in 1936 and larvae were dispersed to several areas outside the Harbour, but widespread breeding did not occur in British Columbia until 1942. Spatfall was extensive throughout the Strait of Georgia and even into many of the inlets which border the Strait. No spatfall occurred north of the Yuculta Rapids—Seymour Narrows area at the northern end of the Strait or south of the Gulf Islands area because of cold water barriers. In 1958, the largest successful general breeding of Pacific oysters occurred, with another smaller one in 1961 of about the same intensity as the one in 1942. Sporadic small breedings have occurred in local areas since then, but they have been minor. Some breeding has also occurred in Barkley and Clayoquot sounds on the west coast of Vancouver Island. However, the few major breedings and the erratic minor ones have been too inconsistent to provide the industry with a reliable and plentiful supply of seed.

Initially, seed was imported annually from Japan. Importations began in 1925 with 20 cases of seed and increased to about 5 400 cases in 1951; the last importation was in 1977. In all, over 625 million seed oysters were imported during this period. However, this source of seed has since become too expensive and unreliable for the industry.

An area within British Columbia which had consistent large-scale Pacific oyster breeding was required to supply the industry with its seed requirements. In 1948, just such an area was discovered. Pendrell Sound lies in the northeast part of the Strait of Georgia and due to local oceanographic conditions, has regular breedings of Pacific oysters. Since monitoring began in 1949, there have only been three breeding failures in this particular area. More recently, two other areas, Hotham Sound and Pipestem Inlet, were found to have fairly consistent breedings and now serve as back-up areas for Pendrell Sound. These three areas are providing inexpensive, reliable and abundant Pacific oyster seed for the industry.

Development of oyster hatcheries has provided the industry with further assurance of a steady seed supply. Initially hatcheries provided individual seed oysters but these proved difficult to handle and were not widely accepted by the industry. Attempts were made to settle larvae on cultch but this was expensive. A recent development has proven to be more successful. Hatcheries now sell eyed-larvae that are ready to settle within 24 hours. Growers construct their own setting tanks, fill them with water that is heated to about 25–30°C, put cultch in the tanks and add the larvae which settle on the cultch within 24 hours. Spat are left in the tank for up to 1 week and are then transferred to an open environment.

The British Columbia oyster industry is primarily a culture or farming operation employing three basic culture techniques: intertidal bottom, near-bottom, and off-bottom culture.

Intertidal bottom culture produces the major portion of British Columbia oysters. In this method, seed is either spread directly on growing areas or more ideally, held for a year on seed ground which has a firm bottom and is high up in the intertidal area. At the end of the year it is spread lower in the intertidal area on grow-out ground, and harvested after at least another 2 years. Good substrate is necessary in grow-out areas; it should be a firm sand–gravel to produce oysters that have well-cupped lower valves and good quality meats.

Near-bottom culture is generally used in areas where the bottom is marginal or soft and takes advantage of the fact that when oysters are cultured off the bottom, they have higher growth and survival rates. Stakes, plastic umbrellas, near-bottom longlines, and racks hold the oyster clutch with seed off the bottom. A marketable oyster can be produced in two growing seasons using this method.

In off-bottom culture, oysters are suspended in deep water and use is made of the entire water column; this is the type of culture used exclusively in Japan and Korea. Cultch with seed is strung at intervals on wire or rope which is suspended from rafts or floating longlines anchored in deep water. The oysters are continually submerged and feed and grow continuously when water temperatures and food concentrations are suitable. Predation is much reduced since the oysters are not touching the bottom. Oysters grown using this system may be harvestable in two growing seasons.

Another type of off-bottom culture used in British Columbia is tray culture. Individual seed oysters are placed in trays and suspended from rafts or floating longlines. The trays are cleaned periodically so that single, well-shaped oysters of high quality are produced.

The oyster industry is centered in the southern part of the coast, mostly in the Strait of Georgia (Fig. 16). The Baynes Sound region between Denman and Vancouver islands produces about 70% of total annual oyster production in the province. Limited production

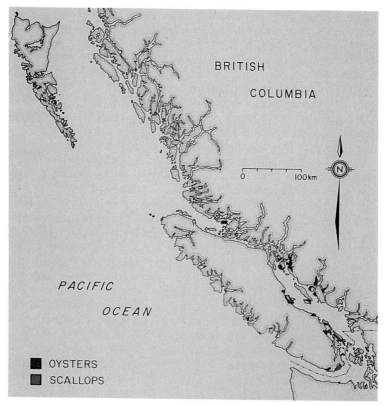

FIG. 16. The spatial distribution of oyster and scallop harvesting in British Columbia.

occurs in some inlets on the west coast of Vancouver Island.

Commercial operations are mostly small family enterprises and the majority of leases are under 10 ha. The number of lease holders has increased with time; in 1983 there were 144 leases covering an area of 1 346 ha. Approximately 300 people are employed by the industry, some on a part-time basis.

Oyster production has fluctuated greatly in the past 40 years (Appendix, Fig. B). Peak production was in 1963, but while landings have decreased, the value of the industry has increased.

In British Columbia, ownership of intertidal and saltwater areas is vested in the Crown. To use intertidal ground or the water column for oyster culture, growers must obtain a lease from the Lands Branch of the Government of British Columbia, which regulates rental of public lands. Growers are responsible for making diligent use of the area, paying rent and providing production figures to monitoring agencies. If a grower fails to make diligent use of the area or fails to keep the area in a clean and safe condition, the area reverts back to the Crown for public use. Management of oyster resources in British Columbia is by the Marine Resources Section, of the B.C. Ministry of Environment.

While most oyster landings are from leases, some commercial and all recreational harvesting of oysters comes from wild oyster populations on unleased foreshore areas. In the commercial industry this harvest has been most significant in years following widespread natural spawning. Commercial harvest of wild populations can only be undertaken under permit issued by the Marine Resources Section. Areas are surveyed to determine the amount of oysters that can be harvested prior to issuing a collection permit. This procedure assures that only acceptable quality oysters reach the commercial market and that sufficient quantities of wild oysters are retained for the recreational fishery.

The future of the British Columbia oyster industry is promising. Although the amount of suitable bottom for oyster culture in the southern part of the province is limited, ideal conditions exist for floating culture. With this technique, the yield per hectare can be increased up to 25 times over that of bottom culture. A conservative estimate of annual production from 610 ha suitable for floating culture in the Strait of Georgia is between 70 000 to 110 000 t round weight. To achieve this potential production, every effort must be made to intensify culture in existing intertidal areas, to encourage adoption of the best growing techniques by industry, to preserve a high quality environment for growing oysters, and to provide longer-term leases.

Scallops

Thirteen species of scallops are found in British Columbia coastal waters, but nine are rare or occur in deep water, and consequently are of interest only to shell collectors or biologists. Four species are either large enough or are found in sufficient abundance to elicit enquiries about establishment of a commercial fishery: weathervane, *Patinopecten caurinus*; rock, *Crassadoma gigantea*; pink, *Chlamys rubida*; and spiny scallops, *C. hastata*, (Fig. 17).

FIG. 17. British Columbian scallops. Clockwise from upper left: pink (*Chlamys rubida*), spiny (*C. hastata*), weathervane (*Patinopecten caurinus*), rock (*Crassadoma gigantea*).

Weathervane scallops — Weathervane scallops are large and can attain a shell diameter of 230 mm. The upper left valve is reddish to yellow−brown in colour with prominent ridges radiating from the umbone to the ventral margin; the lower valve is white to light brown with similar ridges. Distribution in British Columbia is intermittent; a small population occurs in the Gulf Islands area and another in McIntyre Bay off the northeast coast of the Queen Charlotte Islands. Populations in both areas are small. Scattered individuals are found in other areas along the coast in depths from 20 to 200 m, mostly on sand or mud bottom. Under normal conditions, weathervane scallops lie on the bottom on their right (lower) valve with the two valves separated 10−15 mm at the ventral margins. If the scallop is disturbed, the mantle and tentacles are quickly withdrawn and the valves are snapped shut.

One interesting feature of scallops, which is unusual among bivalves, is their ability to swim. Swimming results from a jet action. The valves are opened and water taken in, the valves and mantle are closed and water is forced out through the incurrent and excurrent openings. The scallop shoots forward in a direction away from the hinge, and then the process is repeated; the scallop seems to be taking bites out of the water as it swims. It can also move backward, i.e. hinge first, and in this case water is forced out through the mantle at the ventral edge.

The life history of scallops is similar to that described for the Pacific oyster. Sexes are separate but are readily distinguishable when the gonads are ripe; the male gonad is creamy white in colour, while the female's is red. Time of spawning varies with species. Weathervane scallops in the Gulf Islands spawn in May−June but recruitment appears low since the population is small. Growth of weathervane scallops in the Gulf Islands is fairly rapid; animals 120 mm in height are about 4 years old.

Rock scallops — Rock scallops are large and massive and can attain a shell height of 250 mm. The valves are quite irregular in shape and the outer surface is sculptured with strong radiating ribs, brown−green−grey in colour. Frequently the valves are pitted with holes of boring animals and encrusted with animal and plant growth. Internally, the hinge area is deep purple, hence the common name, purple-hinged rock scallop. In early life-history stages, rock scallops are free swimming, as are other scallops, but when about 25 mm shell height, they attach to a rock and remain there for life. Rock scallops occur throughout the coastal area but are not particularly abundant in any one place. They are found mostly on rocky shores and are essentially subtidal, occurring at only the lowest intertidal level to depths of 80 m. Spawning in southern waters probably occurs in June−July. Initial growth is fairly rapid but slows after they attach to rocks and become massive.

Pink and spiny scallops — Pink and spiny scallops are small species, rarely attaining shell heights greater than 85 mm. The color of the upper valve of spiny scallops can be quite variable, from white through yellow to brown and red, often with bands of white. The bottom valve is usually white with some pale colour. Frequently the upper valve is encrusted with sponge. The upper shell of pink scallops is usually pink−red and has numerous fine ridges radiating from the umbone to the ventral margin of the shell. Spiny scallops have several prominent and numerous small ridges, which are studded with short spines, radiating from the umbone to the ventral margin. Both species occur throughout British Columbia although distribution is discontinuous. They can occur in small dense local beds and are usually found in areas of strong current on firm, gravel or rock bottom. Pink scallops occur somewhat deeper than spiny scallops, 5−200 m compared to 5−150 m. The exact period of spawning is unknown. Growth is slow; animals 75 mm in shell height are about 4 years old. Both pink and spiny scallops are quite active and are frequently observed smimming. After they have moved to another location they re-attach themselves to rock surfaces with byssus.

A large valuable scallop fishery for the sea scallop, *Placopecten magellanicus*, exists on the east coast of Canada and enquiries are often received about the possibility of establishing a similar fishery on the west coast. Interest is further enhanced by a small weathervane scallop fishery in Alaska and a brief, intensive fishery for this species off Oregon in 1981. Scallops are occasionally caught by British Columbia fishermen in trawls or on groundlines, stimulating interest in the possibility of a scallop fishery in British Columbia. Periodic attempts have been made to commercially harvest weathervane scallop populations off the Queen Charlotte Islands and in the Gulf Islands, but these have all been abandoned because of poor catches. An interesting phenomenon of the Queen Charlotte population is that large numbers of weathervane scallops are frequently washed ashore on the beaches east of Masset, particularly on North Beach after severe winter storms, and these are collected by local people for home use and local sale.

Extensive surveys were undertaken in 1960 and 1961 to assess scallop resources along the coast, but results were disappointing. The small weathervane scallop populations off the Queen Charlotte Islands and in the Gulf Islands area were redefined but few scallop concentrations were found in any other areas along the coast, in spite of numerous reports from fishermen of scallops occurring in their catches. Consequently, a sustained fishery for weathervane scallops in British Columbia does not appear likely. There is the possibility that one or two strong year-classes that could support a brief, intensive fishery may settle in an offshore area, as occurred off Oregon, but this would be an unusual event.

Results of several years' study of the Gulf Island weathervane scallop population have shown that it is not large. Underwater observations with the research submersible *Pisces* indicated the population was about 1.3 scallops per 100 square metres. The lack of old shell in dragging work shows the population has never been extensive. The population is too small to support a continuous fishery.

Rock scallops do not lend themselves to a dragging type fishery since they occur subtidally and are firmly cemented to rocks. They can be harvested only by divers, but their sparse distribution and the fact that they must be chipped off rocks probably precludes any commercial fishery. Present regulations prohibit collection of rock scallops for commercial purposes and a bag limit regulates the number that can be taken in the recreational fishery. While coastwide landings of rock scallops are probably not large, relatively few divers can easily remove most of the scallops from specific areas.

Small, localized concentrations of pink and spiny scallops support minor commercial fisheries (Fig. 16), with harvest either by divers or small drags. To date, annual landings have been minor, 25 t in 1985. Traditionally, only the scallop adductor muscle is eaten in North America, although in Europe the roe is also eaten. The small size of these two species has encouraged local marketing of the whole animal. Development of this fishery will depend upon both abundance of spiny and pink scallops found along the coast and the degree to which markets for whole scallops can be developed.

Recently, high market prices for scallops and the impressive success in culturing scallops achieved by the Japanese has stimulated interest in evaluating the potential for scallop culture in British Columbia. Scallop culture is practised in other parts of the world but not as successfully as in Japan, where production increased from about 10 000 t whole weight in 1970 to over 120 000 t in 1980. It is predicted that Japanese production will ultimately reach 500 000 t annually.

Experimental work is currently underway to investigate the feasibility of culturing the four British Columbia species mentioned above and two exotic species, the Japanese scallop (*Patinopecten yessoensis*) and the Atlantic sea scallop (*Placopecten magellanicus*). Of the four native species, major emphasis is on weathervane and rock scallops since they are large and have fairly rapid growth rates. Considerable emphasis is also being placed on the Japanese scallop since it is large, has a rapid growth rate and is widely cultured in Japan. Brood stock of exotic species is brought into the laboratory and bred under quarantine conditions to reduce the possibility of introducing pests, parasites and diseases into British Columbian waters.

A major problem in establishing a culture operation with any species of scallop is the development of a consistent and plentiful supply of seed. Limited amounts of natural seed of all four local species can be collected but probably not in sufficient quantities to permit viable large-scale commercial culture. Initially, seed will have to be raised in hatcheries and work is currently directed towards developing technology for the production of sufficient hatchery seed for commercial operations.

Paralytic shellfish poisoning

Although the concentration of natural toxins in filter-feeding clams, mussels, and oysters does not appear to be something which man can control, its potentially serious nature and widespread prevalence warrants some discussion.

Shellfish become unsuitable for human consumption primarily as a result of two factors — sewage pollution and paralytic shellfish poisoning, or PSP. Polluted animals have a high bacterial content, necessitating an on-going harvesting closure in some coastal locations close to urban areas. In other areas, both molluscs and water quality are monitored regularly by fisheries staff to ensure that bacterial counts do not exceed a safe level. However, as polluted molluscs cleanse themselves fairly quickly when placed alive in clean water, the solution to the problem of sewage contamination is relatively easy to correct.

The same cannot be said for PSP. The term "red tide", often used in conjunction with PSP, is derived from the coloured pigments in the microscopic, one-celled organisms (dinoflagellates) which cause

PSP. When cells are present in high densities, or blooms, they may discolour the water. Depending upon the specific organism involved, this discolouration of the water can be any colour, including red occasionally.

Some dinoflagellate species are harmless, others can kill marine animals, and still other species cause PSP in warm-blooded animals without obviously harming the marine organisms which feed upon them. In British Columbia, two species which appear most frequently in blooms are *Gymnodinium splendors* and *Noctiluca scintillans*, both of which are harmless. Toxic dinoflagellates on the Pacific coast are *Protogonyaulax acatenella* and *P. catenella*, species which normally occur in low densities along the coast throughout the year. It is only when sufficiently high densities of *Protogonyaulax* occur, usually in the summer, that filter-feeding molluscs feeding on them may become toxic by extracting and accumulating the toxin from individual dinoflagellates.

PSP toxin is one of the most potent poisons known, affecting warm-blooded animals by disrupting transmission of nerve impulses. Initial symptoms of PSP usually are tingling of the lips and tongue, later followed by similar sensations in the fingers and toes and loss of voluntary movement and impaired breathing. There is no known antidote.

Conditions which cause local populations of dinoflagellates to become concentrated in abundance are a combination of biological, hydrographic and meteorological processes. Such an occurrence cannot be predicted and because blooms are often of short duration and of limited area, the only reliable way of establishing the safety of filter-feeding molluscs for consumption is to regularly sample and check them for the presence of toxins. This is practical for the more intensively fished areas. However, for more remote, geographically isolated areas where regular sampling is difficult, or impossible, blanket closures for bivalve harvesting have been introduced to maximize public safety.

The standard procedure for evaluating toxicity is to extract any toxin present from a known quantity of mollusc tissue and inject diluted quantities into living mice. The time it takes the mice to react to possible lethal levels of toxin is noted and used to calculate toxicity levels. The lowest concentration of toxin which can be detected by the standard mouse test is 32 micrograms (μg) per 100 g of shellfish tissue. Toxic clams have occasionally been shown to have upwards of 20 000 μg of toxin per 100 g of shellfish tissue. Human sensitivity to poison varies considerably between individuals; some people may show symptoms of poisoning with a dose of 400−500 μg of toxin. With a dose of 2000 μg of toxin, some fatalities may occur.

PSP closures are established whenever toxicity values of shellfish exceed 80 μg of toxin per 100 g of shellfish. Warnings of closures in effect are posted at wharves, marinas, post offices and on beaches. No poisonings in British Columbia have occurred recently from eating commercially harvested shellfish, which are monitored closely for toxicity.

All filter-feeding molluscs may become toxic; this excludes cephalopods (squid and octopus) and herbivorous grazing snails such as abalone which do not filter-feed or prey on filter feeders. Some predatory snails such as whelks and moon snails, which eat filter-feeding molluscs, may in turn concentrate the poison and become toxic. Crab and shrimp are not toxic in British Columbia. Not all filter-feeding species become toxic at the same rate or to the same degree. The rate at which the toxin is excreted may also vary among mollusc species.

Toxic dinoflagellate blooms usually last for about a week and for all harvested bivalve species, the amount of concentrated toxin begins to decline when the *Protogonyaulax* bloom disappears. All species of bivalve, except the butter clam, *Saxidomus giganteus*, become toxin-free in 4−6 weeks, while the latter may retain some toxicity for up to 2 years after exposure. In butter clams, toxins are concentrated in the gills and the siphon (neck), where the toxin is released slowly. The pigmented tip of the siphon of a butter clam is its most poisonous tissue. The adductor muscle meat of free-swimming scallops is never toxic, although other tissues may be. The adductor muscle of rock scallops in California has been recorded as being toxic on occasion.

Octopus and Squid

Octopus

The Class Cephalopoda includes the most active and specialized molluscs, and living species are divided into three groups: the nautuloids, which have a chambered shell; the squid and cuttlefish, which have an internal shell and are discussed in the following section of this publication; and the octopods, which have no shell. The name of this class is derived from the close union of the head with the foot. The foot has become divided to produce two new organs: a series of prehensile tentacles and a muscular funnel. The tentacles are spread completely about the head so that the mouth now lies at their centre and the funnel lies behind the head at the posterior side of the animal where the mantle cavity is situated.

Octopods are the more demersal, or bottom living, of the cephalopods, and have a rounded body and no fins (Fig. 18). Their eight, equal-length tentacles are linked by a web around the mouth and are organs for exploration, attack, holding of prey, and locomotion. Octopods are proficient but not fast jet-swimmers. Each individual is either male or female and dies after one breeding season.

Although 16 species of octopods are found in the eastern Pacific, only three have been recorded in British Columbia; the giant Pacific octopus, *Octopus dofleini*, and the smaller *O. rubescens* and *O. leiodema*. As *O. dofleini* is the only species which is exploited commercially in British Columbia, the remainder of this chapter will be concerned only with this species. Its range extends from northern California to Japan.

In all species of the genus *Octopus*, the third right arm of the male is modified for transferring sperm to the female. In the giant octopus, about 15 cm of the length of this arm has no suckers, and this feature can be used to sex individuals. In addition, the edge of the web on

FIG. 18. The giant octopus, *Octopus dofleini*. (Copyright R. Harbo).

the third right arm of males is folded over to form a longitudinal groove to assist in sperm transfer.

Male sex organs are very complex but, generally speaking, the sperm is encased in a sperm tube which is then coiled into one end of a larger tube called a spermatophore. Mature males may have about eight spermatophores, each about 60 cm long. During copulation, a spermatophore is extended through a penis-like organ into the longitudinal groove of the web. It moves down the groove to the tip of the modified arm, which the male then uses to deposit the spermatophore under the mantle of the female in one of her two oviducts. Exposure of the spermatophore to salt water during mating causes a chemical reaction which ejects the sperm tube inside it through the end of the spermatophore which by then is in the oviduct of the female, thereby releasing the sperm inside the female.

While spawning appears to occur throughout the year, it appears to be most prevalent during the fall. Female octopuses lay 30 000 – 100 000 eggs and brood them for 5 – 6 months on the roof of their dens, at depths ranging from 13 to 30 m. Females do not feed during this time, and consequently die from starvation shortly after, or occasionally even before, the eggs hatch. The eggs hatch over a 40 – 60 day period. The larvae, about 7 mm in length at hatching are planktonic, swimming continuously in the upper water layer for about 2 months before they settle to the sea bottom and adopt a benthic lifestyle. Very little of the biology of young octopuses is known, but because a few individuals have been collected in shallow, inshore water, it has been suggested that this is where they primarily reside. Growth is relatively rapid with little apparent difference in growth rate between the sexes. They reach a weight of 1 kg in about a year and about 12 kg after 18 months. Males in British Columbia mature at about this weight, but continue to grow to about 25 kg. Females reach sexual maturity at a weight of about 20 kg. Reproduction may begin at 2 years of age but more commonly at 3 years, although a few individuals may take as long as 4 or 5 years. Little is known about their reproductive biology but while females likely only mate once, males can probably mate a number of times. The life span of both sexes is 3 – 5 years.

As octopuses start entering fishing traps at about 1 year of age, it is the life history of these larger individuals that is best understood. In Hokkaido, Japan, octopuses weighing over 1 kg make two seasonal onshore – offshore migrations a year, and there is some evidence that this is the case with immature octopuses in British Columbia as well.

In general, the populations are in deep water from February through April and from August through October, and in shallow water from May through July and November through January. During migrations, octopuses may swim at the surface or at mid-water depths as well as crawl along the bottom.

Octopuses will eat just about any animal they can catch. In general, they are nocturnal predators. Analysis of food remains found at den entrances in British Columbia indicates that their diet includes crabs, clams, cockles, abalone, and moon snails. In Japan, octopuses have been shown to also eat flatfish, sandlance, sculpins, shrimp, fish eggs, sea cucumbers, sea squirts, sea stars, squid and other octopods. The main predators of octopus include seals, sea lions, sea otters, dogfish, lingcod, flatfish, and larger octopuses.

As larger octopuses are most frequently found in dens during the day, it has been suggested that abundance of octopuses in a particular area is related to the availability of lairs. This is the basis behind many of the worlds' trap fisheries for octopus. In British Columbia, octopus can be fished using open, unbaited traps. A recent study of the potential for an octopus fishery off Tofino on the west coast of Vancouver Island indicated that the most effective trap design was a large, cedar box trap (Puget Sound design). Fishing was most successful in deep water (80–100 m) during the winter. Catches from inshore traps were relatively low and variable in yield. Trap type, fishing location and time of year were important factors influencing fishing success. Most octopuses caught in traps were males, and at inshore locations were less than 9 kg in weight. In offshore locations, there was more size variation, with individuals ranging from 3 to 18 kg in weight. However catches do not seem large enough to sustain a commercial trap fishery with traditional markets.

The octopus fishery in British Columbia is relatively small, ranging from 18 to 71 t in recent years (Appendix 1, Fig. B), mostly as by-catch in shrimp and groundfish trawling. In contrast, in Hokkaido, Japan, octopus fishing alternated with flatfish during the 1960's as the most valuable fishery resource. From 1956 to 1962, an average of 20 900 t of octopus (mostly the giant Pacific octopus) was landed annually.

In British Columbia, octopus appears to be an underutilized resource. The only fishery regulation is a limitation on the use of some chemicals and sharp-pointed tools in their capture, since the use of such equipment often injures or kills octopus without capturing them.

Since octopus are not extensively fished in British Columbia, their present abundance presumably reflects the existing carrying capacity of the habitat. How this relates to a maximum sustainable yield from an area is not clear, but in Japan, it has been found that the management strategy of increasing the number of refuges on the bottom has increased yield.

The main Canadian market for octopus is as bait for fishing other fish species, and for direct human consumption. It makes a good bait because its firm flesh allows it to stay on a hook for a relatively long time. However, its greatest price is achieved when it is sold as a high quality food for humans. Except for the viscera, beak and eyes, the whole octopus can be consumed. Its flesh is low in fat and although some method of tenderizing is usually necessary, this can readily be accomplished by pounding, pressure cooking or slicing the cooked meat in thin pieces.

Squid

Of the 17 species of squid recorded in British Columbia waters, only four appear to have commercial potential. These are the opal squid, *Loligo opalescens*; the red squid, *Berryteuthis magister*; the nail squid, *Onychoteuthis borealijaponica*; and the flying squid, *Ommastrephes bartrami*.

Loligo are frequently seen in well-illuminated inshore areas at night and are found from the intertidal zone to a depth of 250 m. This species ranges from the southern Gulf of Alaska to Ila Cedros, Mexico, and has been most extensively exploited to date off Oregon and California. *Berryteuthis* is found from the surface to approximately 4 600 m depth and appears to spend most of its time near the ocean floor. It ranges from the Bering Sea to Monterey, California, and is not presently exploited commercially in the eastern Pacific. *Onychoteuthis* is found along the continental shelf where it inhabits a depth of approximately 400 m during the day and comes to the surface during darkness. It is distributed from Oregon to the Gulf of Alaska and as far west as the Sea of Japan and the Okhotsk Sea. This species is not commercially fished off North America. *Ommastrephes* prefers waters around $15-16°C$ or warmer and is common in tropical and subtropical waters throughout the Pacific. It is an offshore species and seldom comes within 50 km of the British Columbian coast. However, warm subtropical waters generally extend northwards well into Canadian offshore waters during the summer months and this species can be commercially exploited at that time. There is a major Japanese fishery for flying squid across the entire north Pacific.

FIG. 19. The flying squid, *Ommastrephes bartrami*.

Squid are molluscs which inhabit the water column, living as vora-
cious predators on both fish and smaller squid. They have cylindrical
shaped bodies with two lateral fins at their tapered, posterior end (Fig.
19). The head has two well-developed eyes, and eight arms and two
tentacles surround the mouth, which has a parrot-like beak. The
tentacles have both suckers and hooks, and their pattern of distribu-

51

tion and characteristics vary depending on the species. Behind the head, in the mantle cavity, is a funnel-like siphon which, by the direction in which it points, allows the animal to control its swimming movements. Swimming is carried out both by flapping of the lateral fins and by rapid contractions of the mantle, which forces water out of the mantle cavity through the siphon. Protective colouration is provided by groups of pigmented cells called chromatophores, which make the animal lighter or darker in colour. Squid, like octopus, can also eject ink which may confuse predators and facilitate escape when attacked.

Little is known about the life history of most squid species. However, because of its inshore and shallow water distribution, the biology of *Loligo* has been studied relatively thoroughly and is described here. In British Columbia, mating can take place year around although the major spawning period is between February and August. After fertilization the female deposits her eggs in 20−30 translucent, finger-like egg cases, each containing 180−300 eggs, that are attached to the sea bottom in sheltered locations, usually on flat areas of mud or sand. Egg development can take up to 3 months. After hatching, the young squid live for the first few days on nourishment from the yolk sac. Early prey appear to be tiny crustaceans in the plankton. The young squid grow rapidly, remaining in the surface plankton until they reach a mantle length of about 4 centimetres, at which time they move nearer to the sea floor. When a mantle length of approximately 8 cm is attained, young squid begin to school with older individuals and feed on fish, crustaceans and smaller squid. Sexual maturity can be reached at 1 year of age and the total lifespan is estimated to be less than 2 years. Death occurs soon after spawning.

Squid are preyed upon by other squid and numerous species of fish including salmon, dogfish, hake, mackerel, bonita, albacore, lingcod, halibut, and tuna. Ratfish have been reported to prey on squid in spawning schools, and marine mammals including whales, porpoises, dolphins, sea lions, fur seals, and harbour seals are also known to be predators. A variety of sea birds feed on squid as well, especially when the squid are in spawning congregations.

Although a substantial fishery for *Loligo* occurs in waters off the west coast of the United States, relatively little fishing occurs in British Columbia. In 1984, 25 vessels reported catches of 69 t of squid. Fishing is carried out at night in shallow water areas using purse seines which are deployed after bright lights have been used to attract schools of spawning squid. Individual squid range in weight from 14

FIG. 20. Hauling-in of a 121 mm gillnet laden with flying squid in an exploratory research fishery in offshore Canadian waters.

to 70 g. Most of the catch is frozen quickly and sold for bait to crab and blackcod fishermen. Relatively little has been used for human consumption in British Columbia. Squid are sometimes caught as by-catch in groundfish trawls and in salmon and herring seines.

In Japan, red and nail squid are fished using jigging machines and bright lights, while flying squid are usually fished with submerged gillnets. Commercial vessels in the Japanese flying squid fishery deploy up to 50 km of gillnet per night and, in an exploratory research study in Canadian waters in 1985, daily landings of up to 1086 kg per kilometre of net deployed were obtained (Fig. 20). This level of return may support viable commercial exploitation by Canadian fishermen and over the next few years, it is hoped that such exploitation will be actively explored.

Squid is still considered an unusual food in North America, although people of many ethnic groups consider it a delicacy. Development of a squid fishery in British Columbia could supply markets in the Orient and, with proper market development, increased local demand seems possible. Stocks appear large enough for further commercial exploitation and interest in these currently underutilized species is increasing as fishermen expand their investigation of alternate fisheries.

CRUSTACEANS

Crustaceans are predominately aquatic and are closely related to spiders and insects. Common characterics include bilateral symmetry; an external skeleton composed of a continuous cuticle; a body generally divided into a head, thorax and abdomen; and jointed appendages.

Crabs

Although 35 species of crabs are found on Canada's Pacific coast, only five species are large enough to be significantly exploited. The Dungeness crab (*Cancer magister*) is the commercial crustacean most commonly found in shallow water in British Columbia. To most people, Dungeness crab (Fig. 21) is identified with the Pacific coast of North America in much the same way as lobster is to Atlantic Canada and New England. Dungeness crabs are highly prized by both commercial and recreational fishermen and while landings have declined over the past decade (Appendix, Fig. C), they are still significant, with a reported value of $4.6 million in 1984. The next most familiar species is the red rock crab, *C. productus*, which supports a small sport fishery and which can be distinguished from Dungeness crab by the black tips of its claws and its redder colouration. There has been a small commercial fishery for the deep-water, golden king crab, *Lithodes aequispina*, in the Observatory Inlet complex, and the shallower-water, red king crab, *Paralithodes camtschatica*, is occasionally fished in northern inlets. However, in recent years there have been few commercial landings of either of these king crab species. Exploratory surveys have been conducted for the tanner crab, *Chionoecetes bairdi*, in recent years but no significant commercially exploitable quantities were located.

Dungeness crab have a maximum shell width of about 230 mm and a weight of about 2 kg. The range of distribution for this species extends from the Aleutian Islands, Alaska, to Monterey Bay, California and from the intertidal to a depth of 180 m. It is most abundant on sand but is also present in mud and gravel areas. Dungeness crab spend much of their time buried in the sediment, and to facilitate breathing, have numerous "hairs" around the main water inlets to the gill chambers, located at the base of the claws and rear legs, which function to hold back sand grains.

Mating can occur only when the female crab molts and her shell is flexible enough to open and receive the male's gonopods, or sexual organs. Prior to molting, a male will clasp the female so that their undersides are in close contact, and he will carry her in this way until the female molts. Mating is accomplished with the female on her dorsal surface, or back, and the male directly over her. Breeding usually occurs in summer, while egg laying and fertilization are delayed until the fall. There is some evidence that the sperm remain viable for at least 1 year, so that two or more batches of eggs may be successfully fertilized between matings.

Relatively few female crabs reach commercial size (165 mm carapace width), as energy expenditure after maturity is directed more towards egg production than body growth. A female crab can produce $500\,000 - 1\,000\,000$ eggs annually, which are carried under her abdomen for about $4-5$ months. After hatching, the planktonic larvae molt through five zoeal stages over about 4 months, with the last stage termed a megalopa. The megalopa is an active swimmer and, while it is recognizably a young crab with tiny claws, its abdomen is still elongated like that of a shrimp. After its final larval molt, the young crab settles to the bottom where it will remain for the rest of its life.

Crabs like all arthropods with exoskeletons, can only increase in size by molting, or shedding their skins. Size increment at each molt is generally about 20%, while the frequency of molting is a function of temperature, food availability, body size, sex, and sexual maturity. In the first year of life, young crabs may molt $6-7$ times whereas 4 to 5 year-old crabs may molt only once every 2 or 3 years. In preparation for molting, much of the old shell is reabsorbed and held in the blood to permit rapid hardening of the new shell after molting. A new larger size is attained by the crab's swallowing water and its subsequent absorption through the stomach, causing enlargement of the body. Over the first few months following a molt, this fluid will gradually be replaced by body tissue, which explains why soft-shell crabs have a lower meat yield and softer, more watery flesh.

Sexual maturity in Dungeness crabs is attained after $10-11$ molts or about $2-3$ years of age. Legal size in males is reached after about 4 years. Crab prey on bivalves, crustaceans, and fish and in turn, are eaten by octopus, halibut, dogfish, sculpins, rockfish, and other larger crabs.

The first record of commercial crab fishing in British Columbia was in 1885. According to early reports, fishing began near the population centres of Vancouver, Victoria, and Nanaimo. Later, fishing oper-

FIG. 21. Dungeness crab, *Cancer magister.*

ations spread to the west coast of Vancouver Island and the Queen Charlotte Islands (Fig. 22). In the late 1930's in the Queen Charlottes, and in the early 1950's in the south, fishermen began using stainless steel circular traps (1 m diameter, 0.3 m deep), a style that is still in use today. Landings increased and during the last three decades, annual landings for the whole coast have ranged from 1200 to 2400 t.

Landings from individual fishing grounds have fluctuated, with the most major decline occurring in Hecate Strait. In this area, average annual landings decreased in the early 1970's from about 680 t to about 200 t. Fishing effort for crabs has increased over time throughout British Columbia, partially in response to declines in landings of other species. The fleet size has grown from 141 vessels fishing crab in 1976 to 363 vessels in 1983.

Present regulations require the use of an escape opening of 100 mm diameter on each trap to permit small, sublegal crabs to escape. Commercial bait includes clams, squid and fish heads or carcasses. The majority of crab vessels fish 50 to 200 traps, but full-time crab fishermen may fish as many as 1 000 traps, with soak periods varying from 1 – 10 days. In Naden Harbour near Masset, fishermen are restricted by regulation to fishing only ring, or hoop, traps.

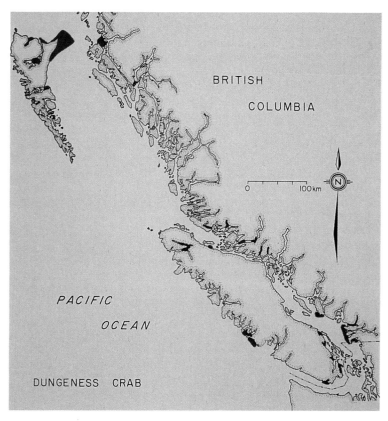

FIG. 22. The spatial distribution of commercial Dungeness crab fisheries in British Columbia.

Historically, most of British Columbia's commercial crab catch has been taken in Hecate Strait and McIntyre Bay, but other areas fished include Boundary Bay, the Fraser River estuary, Burrard Inlet, the Gulf Islands, the west coast of Vancouver Island and Chatham Sound. Crabs are fished in all months of the year, with the main season extending from May to October. Since this in part coincides with the molting period, the fishery is closed during the spring in some areas to maximize yield and reduce injury to the crabs.

Recreational fishermen harvest crabs either with traps, by diving or by dip-netting them at low tide. Use of a jig, gaff, spear, rake, or any sharp point is prohibited.

Management utilizes a minimum carapace width size limit, along with some supportive regulations involving gear usage and local fishery closures. The biological rationale for the size limit is protection of male crabs for 1 year after they reach sexual maturity. The fact that no decline in crab landings has been attributed to overfishing appears to attest to the adequacy of present management and the resilience of this species to heavy exploitation. Little further expansion of the fishery is foreseen, since all stocks are now fully exploited.

Crab culture has never been seriously investigated in British Columbia. Bivalves are more attractive culture candidates and have been given a higher culture research priority. Because crabs are predators, successful culture is likely to be relatively costly if high mortality is to be avoided.

Shrimp

Of the 85 shrimp species recorded in British Columbia, only six are harvested in sport and commercial fisheries. These six species belong to the family of shrimp known as Pandalidae, which is found worldwide and is made up of eighteen genera, of which only two, *Pandalus* and *Pandalopsis*, are found in British Columbia coastal waters. The six species (Fig. 23) which are economically important in British Columbia are: sidestripe (*Pandalopsis dispar*), pink (*Pandalus borealis*), smooth pink (*P. jordani*), coonstripe (*P. danae*), humpback (*P. hypsinotus*), and prawn (*P. platyceros*). Together, their landed value was $4.3 million in 1984 (Appendix 1, Fig. C).

All six species have a peculiar life history trait in common. They display a phenomenon known as protandic hermaphrodism, which means that individuals function initially as mature males when young and as mature females as they become older. It has, however, been demonstrated that it is possible for individuals of some species to bypass the male phase and be female throughout their lives.

Breeding generally takes place in the fall, when the female lays her eggs and attaches them to her abdominal swimming legs, where they are carried until they hatch in the spring. After hatching, the first 2 or 3 months are spent in a number of free swimming larval stages before settling to the bottom as juvenile shrimp. Shrimp normally have a life span of 3 or 4 years. They mature as males in their first or second year of life, remain as such for 1 or 2 years, and then transform into females for their remaining 1 or 2 years.

Sidestripe or giant red shrimp, *P. dispar*, are found in the northeastern Pacific from the Bering Sea to the Oregon coast, mainly on

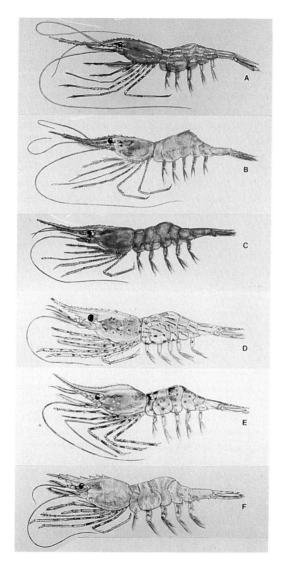

FIG. 23. Commercially exploited shrimp in British Columbia. A. sidestripe, *Pandalopsis dispar*. B. pink, *Pandalus borealis*, C. smooth pink, *Pandalus jordani*. D. coonstripe, *Pandalus danae*. E. humpback, *Pandalus hypsinotus*. F. prawn, *Pandalus platyceros*.

59

a mud bottom. The large antennules and striped abdomen distinguish this shrimp from other species. They are usually harvested by trawl and are fished in a number of small, mixed shrimp fisheries located in Chatham Sound, Burrard Inlet, Stuart Channel and Barkley Sound. They are generally marketed whole and fresh.

Pink or northern shrimp, *P. borealis*, are distinguished by their uniform pink to red coloration and the presence of dorsal spines on both the third and fourth abdominal segments. This shrimp is circumboreal in distribution from the Barents Sea to the North Sea. In the northeastern Pacific, it ranges from the Aleutian Islands to the Columbia River mouth. In British Columbia, it is confined mainly to the mud bottom of mainland inlets. This species is the target of the large shrimp fishery in Alaska. In British Columbia, pink shrimp are exploited mainly in beam trawl fisheries off English Bay and in Chatham Sound.

Smooth pink, ocean, or ocean pink shrimp, *P. jordani*, are very similar to *P. borealis* except that the dorsal spines are absent. The distribution of this species is from Unalaska Island to San Diego, and it is the main target species for the shrimp fisheries off Washington, Oregon and Northern California. In British Columbia, *P. jordani* is found on mud bottom grounds off the west coast of Vancouver Island, in Queen Charlotte Sound, in Stuart Channel and off Comox. These fisheries have been sporadic with the largest landing occurring in 1976 when over 5000 t were taken off the west coast of Vancouver Island. The 1982 landing from the same area was 100 t.

Coonstripe or dock shrimp, *P. danae*, range from Alaska to California. In British Columbia they are found on sandy, gravel and rocky bottoms, generally in areas subject to high tidal flow. The only commercial fishery that presently targets exclusively on this species is a small, winter trap fishery in Sooke Harbour. This area produces between 5 to 50 t in a season, and the product is sold either fresh or cooked to local markets in Vancouver and Victoria. This shrimp is also exploited in the sports fishery, as it is readily fished with ring traps and dip nets near docks and marinas, especially near Sidney.

Humpback, or king shrimp, *P. hypsinotus*, are relatively large shrimp found in the northeastern Pacific from Alaska to Puget Sound in Washington. As the name humpback implies, this shrimp has a distinctively arch-shaped carapace. The only directed fishery for this shrimp occurs in Masset Inlet where it is harvested by both trap and trawl. It is also caught incidentally in a number of inside waters in prawn traps and pink shrimp beam trawl tows. Because of its large

FIG. 24. Prawn, *Pandalus platyceros.*

size, this shrimp is often marketed fresh or frozen whole and is considered by many to be the finest eating of all the local shrimp species.

The largest of all Canadian shrimp species, *P. platyceros*, is commonly referred to as prawn or spot shrimp (Fig. 24). The term prawn has been used in a number of locations for a number of different crustacean species, which often results in confusion as to what is the difference between a shrimp and a prawn. In this instance, there is, in fact, no difference; the term prawn is simply the common name used for British Columbia's largest shrimp species. In the northeastern Pacific, *P. platyceros* ranges from Alaska to California, and as it is generally associated with rocky terrain, is fished primarily with traps.

Prior to 1979, prawn trapping in British Columbia was concentrated in the south coast region. Since 1979, participation in the fishery has increased from about 50 vessels to over 300 vessels in 1984 and the fishery is now widespread (Fig. 25). Vessels are 5 to 35 m in length and fish 40–1500 traps. About 30 trap types are used by fishermen, and differences between traps involve number of tunnel entrances, tunnel size, entrance ring size and mesh size. Fishing methods used also vary considerably with respect to the amount of time the gear is left in the water (usually 3 to 96 h), depth fished

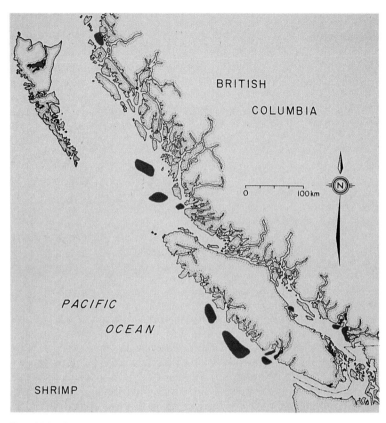

FIG. 25A. The spatial distribution of shrimp fisheries (mostly trawl) in British Columbia.

(between 15 and 250 m), and bait (at least 6 popular types). The recent development of a northern fishery is due to the expansion of markets, overcrowding by fishermen in southern areas, and positive results from exploratory prawn surveys in this area in the late 1970s. The high price paid for prawns makes it the most valuable shrimp species in British Columbia, although the total landed weight of other shrimp species may be greater. Prawns are also the most popular shrimp species for sports fishermen, who are allowed to fish up to four traps at a time.

As indicated above, shrimp fisheries utilize either trawls or traps. The trawl fishery is presently a limited entry fishery, with about 242

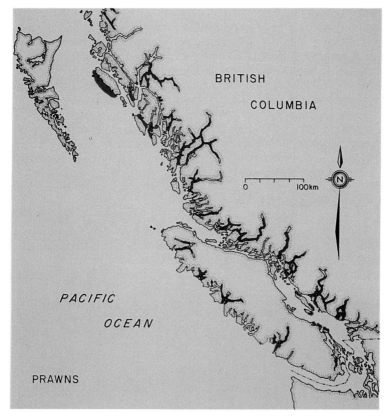

FIG. 25B. The spatial distribution of prawn trap fisheries in British Columbia.

licenses issued in 1985. When implemented, management of trawl fisheries has been based on precautionary quotas.

Trap fisheries presently utilize one of two strategies, depending on the species involved. Prawn are managed by determining a catch per unit effort value for female spawners, which is compared to an acceptable monthly spawner index. When the observed catch value declines to the level of, or below, the expected monthly index, the area is closed to fishing until the end of the egg-bearing period, normally at the end of the following March. This system is logistically difficult to effect, but it is considered to provide conservative management. More cost effective, alternative management approaches are currently being evaluated.

Coonstripe shrimp are managed by means of a quota. The relative abundance of shrimp of different ages is estimated prior to the opening of a seasonal fishery. This information is used to recommend a harvestable quota. This management approach is only practical with relatively small, discrete populations of shrimp because of the difficulties in acquiring sufficient data to yield accurate population estimates.

Shrimp culture, like crab culture, has not been seriously investigated in British Columbia to date because of other priorities. Local species do not at this time appear to have the viable culture potential of tropical penaeid shrimps.

Euphausiids

There are approximately 85 species of euphausiids, 23 of which have been reported in British Columbia waters. Superficially, euphausiids (Fig. 26) bear a close resemblance to shrimps; however, amongst other differences, shrimp have five pairs of unbranched

FIG. 26. A euphausiid, *Euphasia pacifica*, in a dish feeding on a larval herring. The grid in the background is 1 centimetre square.

thoracic legs while euphausiids have six to eight pairs of two-branched thoracic legs. Luminescent organs in the base of the eye stalk, on the second and seventh thoracic limbs, and on the first few abdominal segments are also characteristic of euphausiids. Maximum body length ranges from 6 to 150 mm, depending on the species, but most fall between 10−30 mm in length.

Euphausiids are found throughout the world's oceans, generally where the salinity is greater than 28 parts per thousand. As a group, they comprise the second largest weight, or biomass, of animal life in the ocean, exceeded only by another crustacean group, the copepods. Euphausiids are particularly abundant in subarctic and subantarctic waters, where they are commonly referred to as krill.

In British Columbia, euphausiids are concentrated in areas where the water depth is over 200 m: the outer continental shelf along the west coasts of the Queen Charlotte Islands and Vancouver Island, submarine canyons on the shelf and in some fjords. They tend to form large swarms, in concentrations of up to 40 000 animals m^{-3} in a relatively narrow depth range. At dusk individuals migrate vertically from deep water to the surface to feed, a distance of more than half a kilometre for some species. The depth to which they migrate at dawn is controlled primarily by light level, but total water column depth, temperature and dissolved oxygen concentration may also be important factors. On bright moonlit nights, euphausiids may not migrate all the way to the surface nor form as dense a layer as they do on dark nights. This avoidance of light is thought to help euphausiids avoid predators which might otherwise see them.

Euphausiids are an important food item for many fish, seabirds, baleen whales and seals because of their abundance and tendency to swarm. In British Columbia major predators of euphausiids are herring, hake, walleye pollock and salmon, as well as squid and some pelagic shrimps.

Euphausiids themselves adapt their mode of feeding to utilize a wide variety of foods. Phytoplankton is the major food source of *Euphasia pacifica* in the spring in productive coastal areas, while microzooplankton may be more important in coastal areas during winter and in the offshore oceanic environment.

The life span for most euphausiids in British Columbia waters is about 19 months for males and 22 months for females. Life span increases with latitude; the life span for *E. pacifica* off the California and Oregon coast is 12 months, increasing to approximately 24 months for the same species in the Bering Sea. The primary spawning period extends from early May to mid-July, the time when phytoplankton concentrations are also high. Less intensive spawning may occur sporadically throughout the summer and early fall.

Eggs are fertilized externally from a spermatophore that the male transfers to the female. Females may carry the spermatophores around for several months before the eggs, each about 0.4 mm in diameter, are released. Eggs of most species of euphausiid float free in the plankton for 5−6 days, after which they hatch into the first larval stage, or nauplius. Young euphausiids then pass through 10−23 larval stages over about four weeks before reaching the juve-

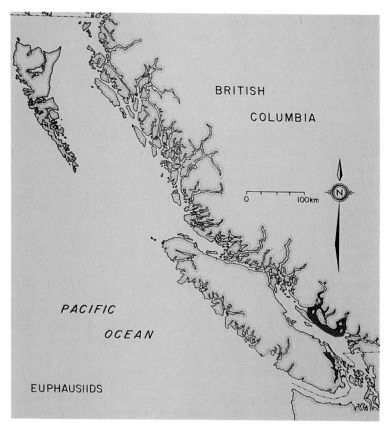

FIG. 27. The spatial distribution of euphausiid fisheries in British Columbia in 1984.

nile stage. Maximum growth rate of juvenile *E. pacifica* in Saanich Inlet occurs during the summer, with individuals growing about 0.1 mm per day. Growth slows in late summer and autumn as animals become mature and food becomes more scarce, and almost ceases during winter.

The fishery for euphausiids in British Columbia began in 1970 with an experimental fishery in the Strait of Georgia. The intent of this inshore fishery was to develop gear and fishing methods for an offshore fishery. However, the fishery, which utilizes small boats and lands catches destined for specialty markets, has not expanded to include offshore stocks. Annual landings have been less than 200 t with fishing taking place primarily in Saanich Inlet, Jervis Inlet and Howe Sound (Fig. 27). Due to marketing problems, the fishery has been sporadic.

In 1976, quotas were established to limit the fishery as a result of concerns about the importance of euphausiids as a valuable source of food for salmonids and other commercial fish species. In the Strait of Georgia the annual catch quota has been set at 453 t, with an open season from November through March. The timing of this fishing season minimizes the incidental capture of large numbers of larval and juvenile fish and early pelagic stages of shrimps and crabs. The total catch quota is estimated to be less than 0.1% of annual euphausiid production in exploited areas.

MARINE PLANTS

Macroscopic marine algae are photosynthetic plants present in intertidal and subtidal waters throughout the world, usually fixed to a substrate. Algae in general are much simpler than land plants and obtain water, nutrients and dissolved gases they need for growth and reproduction directly from the surrounding water medium.

The holdfast, a root-like, sometimes branched structure, acts as an anchor attaching the plant to the substrate. True roots, with absorption and conduction functions, occur only in the more complex terrestrial plants and marine seed plants (e.g. the eel grasses, *Zostera* spp. and surf grasses *Phyllospadix* spp.). The stem-like portion of some algae, called the stipe, contains pigments active in photosynthesis. The leaf-like structures found in large algae, or macrophytes, are called laminae or blades, and are the main organs of photosynthesis and in some cases, reproduction.

All algae contain the green pigment chlorophyll. In addition, some algae have additional red or brown pigments which gives them their distinctive colouration. These auxiliary pigments enable red and brown algae to absorb light from additional portions of the white light spectrum. In general, green algae (chlorophytes) are found shallowest, brown algae (phaeophytes) are found at mid-water depths and red algae (rhodophytes) are found deepest. Most of the world's economically important algae are found at depths shallower than 40 m.

Green algae are most closely related to land plants, and are probably the ancestral stock from which land plants arose. They are most common in tropical and subtropical waters. In brown algae, the green colour is masked by a variety of other pigments which are brown or gold, and their colour ranges from light brown to almost black. There are about 140 species of brown algae in the Pacific Northwest, and brown algae are the most conspicuous group of seaweeds found in British Columbia. The largest species are the kelps, some of which reach lengths up to 25 m and form huge, near-shore kelp forests. Red algae have both red and blue auxiliary pigments, and are represented by about 265 species in the Pacific Northwest.

The life histories of algae are some of the most complex and varied of all plants. Most algae reproduce both sexually and asexually, alternating between these two types of reproduction. Sexual reproduction, involving the union of male and females gametes, produces a generation (sporophyte) which reproduces asexually by means of zoospores. These germinate and grow to form the gamete-producing generation (gametophyte), and the process is then repeated. Green and brown algae have reproductive cells which are capable of swimming, while red algae do not have mobile reproductive cells.

Algae are known to have been used as a source of food as early as 3000 B.C. but in this century, man's use of marine algae has expanded greatly. Today, algae are used directly as food, in medicine, as a fodder and fertilizer, in the production of industrial compounds and most recently, as a source of energy in the production of methane gas. Useage of marine plants by man is briefly summarized below:

Direct Consumption

Although marine plants are frequently eaten, particularly in the Orient, most algae are not a good source of food calories since much cell wall material is indigestible by humans. However, many seaweeds are used for their distinct flavors as condiments in salads and soups, while others are rich in vitamins and minerals.

In Japan and China, where seaweed has been cultured since the 1700's, a substantial culture industry presently exists. Nori, a thin bladed red algae (*Porphyra*), is cultured extensively and is quite nutritious, with about 25% of its dry weight being protein. Since *Porphyra* is high in Vitamin C, it was used historically by the British Navy to prevent scurvy on long voyages.

Kelps, types of brown algae, are large and relatively easily harvested, and in Japan edible kelps are known as "kombu". Kombu is also cultured, and is sold dried for use in soups and stews. Finely shredded or powdered kelp can be used in candies and cakes or taken as a mineral supplement.

At present, North American markets for edible algae are restricted primarily to oriental cuisine and health foods. Interest in algae as a food continues to increase, despite the fact that very little is known about the actual nutritional value to humans of seaweed proteins, carbohydrates and fats. Vitamins and minerals contained in seaweeds are often advocated as dietary supplements.

Industrial Usage

Industrial use of marine plants centers on the long-chained sugars (polysaccharides) found in both red and brown algae. Alginates are extracted from brown algae while agar and carrageenan are extracted from red algae. Algin is composed of long molecules contained in cell walls, and is used in the production of a variety of products such as textiles, charcoal briquets, candy bars, car polishes, cosmetics, dairy products, rubber, etc. Most recently, alginates have been used to make surgical threads which dissolve after a period of time in the body. Alginates are also used to produce a whole blood substitute which is used in emergency transfusions.

Agar is present in commercial quantities in red algae species such as *Gelidium* and *Gracilaria*, both of which occur in British Columbia. Agar is used extensively in the food industry, particularly as a substitute for gelatin, as an anti-drying agent in baked goods, in the manufacture of frozen dairy products such as ice cream and in the preparation of rapid-setting jellies and desserts. In science, it is used as a culture medium in medical and microbiological research.

Carrageenan is used extensively in the food industry to stabilize milk proteins. It is also used in toothpaste, diet foods, insect sprays, and numerous other household products.

Fodder

Algae is fed to pigs, sheep, cattle, and poultry. Animal reproduction, milk production and growth are enhanced by its use. For centuries, seaweeds have been used as a green manure in coastal farming areas in Europe and North America. Today, commercial fertilizers are often made directly from mulched seaweeds. Brown algae helps improve soil structure and increase water retention, and contains trace elements and other essential metabolites.

Medicines

Extracts from various marine plants are used in the pharmaceutical industry as vermifuges, blood anticoagulents and in the treatment of intestinal disorders such as constipation and stomach aches.

In the ocean, marine plants act as a direct food source for many marine herbivores. Sea urchins and abalone, for example, graze the giant kelps *Macrocystis* and *Nereocystis* (Fig. 28). Kelp forests provide an important environment for near-shore animals and often structure the community. Numerous species of fish and invertebrates live beneath the canopy formed by the kelp forest, and kelp may provide a major refuge for juveniles of many commercially important species of fish. These complex interactions between algae and animals in the ecosystem demonstrate the need to maintain a balance between the individual components of the system when managing a natural resource.

Marine plants in British Columbia have long been recognized as an underutilized resource. The waters of the Pacific Northwest contain many economically important species of algae which are utilized as food and by industry in other parts of the world. However, as their ecological importance is not yet well understood, conservative management has been adopted to minimize effects on community structure and the dynamics of other commercial species.

In British Columbia, the major harvest of marine plants is by the herring spawn-in-kelp fishery. Native people have collected seaweed covered with herring eggs (Fig. 29) since prehistoric times. "Gow", as it is known to the Haida people, is a much sought after seasonal food. A small spawn-on-kelp fishery directed at Japanese markets, was

FIG. 28. A near-shore kelp bed in 5–10 m of water. (*Top*) As seen from the water surface. (Bottom) A single plant (*Nereocystis luetkeana*) as seen from the sea bottom. (Copyright R. Harbo, both photographs.)

FIG. 29. Top-grade herring spawn-on-kelp, a blade of *Macrocystis* covered with at least three layers of eggs on each side.

developed in 1975. Today, this fishery is flourishing. Fronds of *Macrocystis* are harvested from the wild and suspended in net pens in which herring are impounded. The herring spawn on the kelp, which is then collected, salted and shipped to Japan. A recent development, termed open-ponding, involves the hanging of fronds from rafts which are pushed into concentrations of naturally spawning fish. In 1984, 28 permit holders produced $4.5 million of spawn-on-kelp product using about 90 t of *Macrocystis*.

RESOURCE MANAGEMENT

In preceding sections specific regulations and management measures adopted for different species have been described. In this section, the structure of the management process for invertebrates is outlined and unique factors affecting general management of invertebrate populations are discussed briefly.

Management of fishery resources is presently carried out by the Field Services Branch, Department of Fisheries and Oceans. Management biologists responsible for Pacific invertebrate fisheries in each of the three regional areas (North Coast, South Coast, and

Fraser River) receive biological advice from Fisheries Research Branch scientists and biologists, and advice on social and economic conditions from other departmental staff, fishermen's representatives and provincial fisheries personnel. In British Columbia, fishery officers have the authority to open and close fisheries in their areas of responsibility. Faecal coliform levels in shellfish grow-out areas are monitored on a regular basis by the Environmental Protection Service of Environment Canada, while the Inspection Division of Field Services Branch has responsibility for monitoring faecal coliforms and paralytic shellfish poisoning in shellfish. If bacteriological or toxicity levels exceed established standards, closures of contaminated areas are immediately recommended to local fishery officers, and permanent closure may be scheduled in regulations.

As fisheries have expanded, fishermen have become more actively involved in the management process and, in many instances, have formed associations to express their collective views. There are presently at least six fishermen's groups dealing with invertebrate species which meet with research and management biologists on a regular basis.

Management data available for invertebrate species differs significantly from that available for finfish species due to a number of unique biological and fishery characteristics. Many invertebrates have limited mobility, and move only a few metres (e.g. bivalves) or perhaps a few kilometres (e.g. octopus, echinoderms, abalone, prawns) during their lives. Dungeness crab and some shrimp species may move somewhat further, but only squid are as mobile as most commercial finfish. This limited mobility means that the impact of exploitation on the population is not spread rapidly throughout the stock. Abundance of legal size individuals in a particular concentration of adults may be depleted but sampling elsewhere in the population will not show this impact. Invertebrates are often located in concentrations, and it is the identification and exploitation of these widely distributed concentrations that permits harvesting in commercial quantities.

Limited mobility also means that most invertebrates do not concentrate their whole population in a few locations at certain times of the year for feeding, migration or spawning, as do salmon, herring, and many groundfish species. It is at such times and locations that many finfish fisheries occur, and the presence of such concentrations greatly facilitates use of conventional stock assessment procedures. In contrast, invertebrate exploitation occurs throughout the coast in most seasons of the year at a relatively low, but continuous, rate.

Surveys to establish a population's status thus must cover a relatively large geographic area. This can be very costly and difficult to effect, and so such surveys are only rarely attempted.

Initially, most invertebrate fisheries were intertidal or nearshore in nature. Until recently, difficulty in transportation of a high quality product meant that the catch was either consumed directly by the local population or processed immediately. The diffuse nature of invertebrate fisheries and relatively small local landings supported the existence of many small processing and marketing companies which explains why many of today's major fish processing companies are only marginally involved with invertebrates. This has made the comprehensive biological sampling of commercial catches relatively expensive and logistically difficult to implement, and has presented problems in the accurate compilation of catch statistics. With the high price paid for many species, sales are often undocumented and not included in official catch statistics.

The recreational fishery, which we know is substantial for some invertebrate species, has also not been studied in detail. Neither the magnitude of landings nor the economic value of this fishery are known.

The widespread, clumped distribution and cryptic nature of most invertebrate species makes determination of total abundance, or biomass, of most species difficult to establish accurately even in a relatively small area. The lack of accurate estimates of total abundance, and, in some cases, catch, has restricted the usefulness of many traditional stock assessment methods. Consequently, biological advice has not been generally used to modify landings on an annual basis, a management strategy which can be applied to many other fisheries. Thus, for most exploited invertebrate species, more passive management is practised, and a minimum size limit below which individuals of a species cannot be retained and/or a conservative, fixed quota, have been main management regulations. For Dungeness crab and intertidal bivalves, the same size limit has been in effect for over 50 years. In its simplest form, size limits are set so that individuals are usually sexually mature for one to two spawnings before their legal exploitation can occur. Because of the relatively high reproductive capacities of many invertebrates, this regulation alone appears to have been sufficient to ensure many species' continued existence. Fluctuations in actual abundance will occur on an annual basis, and landings will reflect the strength of individual year-classes. For most species, fluctuations in abundance appear to be most influenced by environmental rather than fishery factors.

FUTURE DEVELOPMENTS

It is anticipated that invertebrate fisheries will assume greater importance to many fishermen in future years as fishing for more traditional finfish species becomes more competitive. Most populations of traditionally exploited invertebrate species (crab, some clams, abalone, etc.) are now fully exploited and any future increase in their landings will reflect either changes in year-class strength or landed price. Future fishery expansion can thus be in either of two directions: markets will be established or expanded for species which are presently unutilized or underutilized, such as sea urchins, sea cucumbers and flying squid, or new technology such as mariculture will be used to enhance the harvest of species whose natural production is now fully exploited.

Fishery expansion through harvest of new species will largely depend on the ingenuity of entrepreneurs in establishing markets. However, while considerable return can likely be realized in this area, it appears that the greatest potential for expanded invertebrate harvest will come from mariculture. At present, only oysters are being cultured in British Columbia in commercial quantities, with production still well below potential levels. Mussel culture is beginning and production should increase greatly in the near future. Technology to culture abalone and scallops is being developed, and the potential of clam culture is presently under investigation.

Much has been written about the potential for mariculture in recent years. Developments are presently occurring rapidly in such disciplines as population genetics, disease diagnostics and treatment, quality control, nutrition, and animal husbandry. Problems which seemed insurmountable only a few years ago are now being resolved and in many cases, emphasis is on fine-tuning rather than establishing a general methodology. In invertebrates, three general types of culture are possible:

1. Seed or juveniles for culture can be collected in the wild for subsequent grow-out on prepared beaches (relaying) or in suspended culture. This approach is presently the basis of most oyster and all mussel culture in British Columbia.
2. Seed can be produced under controlled conditions in a hatchery with subsequent grow-out in the natural environment. Some oyster and all clam production involves this approach, and it is being considered for abalone and scallop production in the future.

3. Seed production and grow-out can be entirely under controlled conditions. This approach is the most sophisticated technologically and is most utilized with those species which are found at low average densities in the wild. It is being considered for abalone in British Columbia and for American lobster in eastern Canada.

It is not possible to predict which form of culture will be most successful in British Columbia. A great deal depends upon species, site selection, price and market demand and availability of seed. Only through careful planning and practical attempts at culture can methods applicable to our unique environmental conditions be assessed and developed.

There is no biological reason why the development of invertebrate culture in British Columbia cannot approach a level similar to that in Japan, where invertebrate culture is on the same scale as that of finfish. Over the next few decades, expansion of mariculture can be expected to revolutionize invertebrate fisheries in British Columbia. This will constitute a major challenge to fishermen who must adapt to, and involve themselves in, such changes.

ACKNOWLEDGEMENTS

The editors thank F. Bernard, P. Breen, M. Coon, R. Harbo, and J. Watson for reviewing sections of the manuscript, and R. Harbo for a major contribution of copyrighted photographs. All contributors express their appreciation to the many researchers whose published reports over the years have contributed to the information used here in this report.

GLOSSARY

abdomen — the portion of the body composed of a group of similar segments and containing the reproductive organs and posterior portion of the digestive system.

asexual reproduction — any type of reproduction not involving gametes.

benthic — adjective for animals and plants which live on the bottom.

bilateral symmetry — arrangement of body parts so that there are right and left sides, dorsal and ventral surfaces, and front and rear ends.

biomass — total weight of all organisms, or a designated species, in a particular habitat or area.

bivalve — any member of the molluscan Class Pelecypoda; having a shell of two parts (valves) which are joined by a hinge.

byssus — bundle of protein anchorage filaments produced by some marine bivalves.

carapace — dorsal and lateral shield-like plate covering the cephalothorax of some crustaceans.

cephalothorax — body divisions representing a fusion of one or more thoracic segments with the head.

chromatophore — a special cell, usually in the skin, which contains an abundance of pigment granules which are usually capable of being dispersed or concentrated.

circumboreal — a geographical distribution which encompasses all land or marine areas in the colder parts of the northern hemisphere.

colloid — a non-crystalline substance with very large molecules forming a viscous solution with special properties.

cultch — natural or synthetic material used to collect oyster or other bivalve spat.

cuticle — a dead, non-cellular layer secreted by the outer skin layer.

dorsal — the back or upper surface.

endoskeleton — any animal skeleton which is built into the body and gives support and permanent shape to it.

equilateral — equal-sided.

eyestalk — stalk bearing a terminal eye.

exoskeleton — an invertebrate skeleton of variable composition which forms the outermost covering of the body.

fouling — any organism that attaches to submerged objects.

gamete — mature, functional sex cell (egg or sperm) capable of uniting with the alternate sex cell (fertilization).

glycogen — animal starch made of sugar molecules.

gonad — gamete-producing organ in an animal; ovary or testis.

gonopod — a leg modified for reproduction.

hermaphrodite — individual having both male and female reproductive organs functional.

holdfast — the basal attachment organ of an alga.

intertidal — that portion of the sea bottom between high and low tide lines. Chart Datum is the lowest normal tide and height of tide is the vertical distance between the surface of the sea and Chart Datum.

macrophyte — a large plant.

megalops — larval stage of marine crabs which just precedes the adult form.

metamorphosis — period of abrupt transformation from one distinctive stage in the life history to another, e.g. larvae to the adult form.

molt — periodic shedding of the exoskeleton to permit an increase in size.

nekton — collectively, the macroscopic animals suspended in water which move independently of currents.

ossicle — plates, spicules and rods making up the structure of the echinoderm endoskeleton.

periostracum — outermost chitinoid layer of most mollusc shells; protects the underlying calcareous prismatic layer from erosion.

photosynthesis — the process in which light is used by plants to build complex substances from carbon dioxide and water.

plankton — collectively, all those organisms suspended in water which are primarily dependent on currents and other water movements to transport them.

protandry — among hermaphroditic organisms the mature formation of functional sperm before the formation of mature ova.

radial symmetry — body parts arranged around one longitudinal axis.

recruitment — the entry of new individuals into a population through reproduction or into a size category through growth.

roe — swollen ovaries or extruded eggs of some invertebrates.

seed — small bivalves used in cultivation and transplantation.

spat — recently settled bivalves.

species — groups of organisms which actually (or potentially) interbreed and which are reproductively isolated from all other such groups.

spermatophore — capsule or packet formed by some male invertebrates; contains sperm and is usually transferred to the female to facilitate fertilization.

stipe — the stem-like, usually basal part of a thallus.

substrate — the ground or any other solid object to which an animal may be attached, or which it moves about on, or with which it is otherwise associated.

subtidal — that portion of the sea bottom below the low tide line.

test — rigid calcareous skeleton of some echinoderms.

thallus — the whole plant body of an alga or fungus.

thorax — central portion of the body between the head and abdomen.

umbone — beak-like projections on either side of the hinge area in a bivalve mollusc; marks the point of origin of growth in the juvenile bivalve.

valve — one of the two shells in a typical bivalve mollusc.

ventral — under or lower body surface.

year-class — all the young of a species that are produced in one annual spawning season (usually a calendar year).

zoea — one of the early larval stages of marine crabs, usually marked especially by long anterior and dorsal spines.

RELATED READING

Sea Cucumber

HARBO, R. 1982. Diving fishermen. *Diver*, (June) 20–23.

McDANIEL, N. 1982. The giant sea cucumber. *Diver*, (March) 26–27.

MOTTET, M. G. 1976. The fishery biology and market preparation of sea cucumbers. Wash. Dep. Fish. Tech. Rep. 22: 44 p.

SLOAN, N. A. 1986. World jellyfish and tunicate fisheries and the northeast Pacific echinoderm fishery, p. 23–33. *In* G. S. Jamieson and N. Bourne [ed.] North Pacific Workshop on stock assessment and management of invertebrates. Can. Spec. Publ. Fish. Aquat. Sci. 92.

Sea Urchins

ADKINS, B. E., R. M. HARBO, AND P. A. BREEN. 1981. A survey of commercial sea urchin, *Strongylocentrotus franciscanus*, populations in the Gulf Islands. Can. MS Rep. Fish Aquat. Sci. 1618: 41 p.

BERNARD, F. R. 1977. Fishery and reproductive cycle of the red sea urchin, *Strongylocentrotus franciscanus*, in British Columbia. J. Fish. Res. Board Can. 34(5): 604–610.

BREEN, P. A. 1979. The ecology of red sea urchins in British Columbia. Proc. First. Int. Symp. on Coastal Pacific Marine Life, Bellingham, Washington. 3–12 p.

MOTTET, M. G. 1976. The fishery biology of sea urchins in the family Strongylocentrotidae. Wash. Dep. Fish. Tech. Rep. 20.

SIMENSTAD, C. A., J. A. ESTES, AND K. W. KENYON. 1980. Aleuts, sea otters, and alternate stable-state communities. Science 200; 403–411.

SLOAN, N. A. 1986. World jellyfish and tunicate fisheries and the northeast Pacific echinoderm fishery, p. 23–33. In G. S. Jamieson and N. Bourne [ed.] North Pacific Workshop on stock assessment and management of invertebrates. Can. Spec. Publ. Fish. Aquat. Sci. 92.

TEGNER, M. J., AND P. K. DAYTON. 1977. Sea urchin recruitment patterns and implications of commercial fishing. Science 196: 324–326.

Abalone

BREEN, P. A. 1980. Measuring fishing intensity and annual production in the abalone fishery of British Columbia. Can. Tech. Rep. Fish. Aquat. Sci. 947: 49 p.

BREEN, P. A. 1986. Management of the British Columbia fishery for northern abalone (Haliotis kamtschatkana). In G. S. Jamieson and N. Bourne [ed.]. North Pacific Workshop on stock assessment and management of invertebrates. Can. Spec. Pub. Fish. Aquat. Sci. 92.

COX, K. W. 1962. California abalones, family Haliotidae. Calif. Dep. Fish Game, Fish Bull. 118: 133 p.

MOTTET, M. G. 1979. A review of the fishery biology of abalone. Wash. Dep. Fish. Tech. Rep. 37: 81 p.

QUAYLE, D. B. 1971. Growth, morphometry and breeding in the British Columbia abalone (Haliotis kamtschatkana Jonas). Fish. Res. Board Can. Tech. Rep. 279: 83 p.

Geoduck

ANDERSON, A. M. 1971. Spawning, growth, and spatial distribution of the geoduc clam, Panope generosa Gould in Hood Canal, Washington. Ph.D. thesis, University of Washington, Seattle, WA. 133 p.

BREEN, P. A., AND T. L. SHIELDS. 1983. Age and size structure in five populations of geoduc clams (Panope generosa) in British Columbia. Can. Tech. Rep. Fish. Aquat. Sci. 1169: 62 p.

GOODWIN, L. 1976. Observations on spawning and growth of subtidal geoducs (Panope generosa Gould). Proc. Nat. Shellfish Assoc. 65: 49–58.

HARBO, R. M., AND S. D. PEACOCK. 1983. The commercial geoduck fishery in British Columbia, 1976–1981. Can. MS Rep. Fish. Aquat. Sci. 1712: 40 p.

SHAUL, W., AND L. GOODWIN. 1982. Geoduck (*Panope generosa*: Bivalvia) age as determined by internal growth lines in the shell. Can. J. Fish. Aquat. Sci. 39: 632–636.

SLOAN, N. A., AND S. M. C. ROBINSON. 1986. Age and gonad development in the geoduck clam *Panope abrupta* (Conrad) from southern British Columbia, Canada. J. Shellfish Res. 4: (in press).

Intertidal Clams

ANDERSON, G. J., M. B. MILLER, AND K. K. CHEW. 1982. A guide to manila clam aquaculture in Puget Sound. Washington Sea Grant, Univ. of Washington. WSG-82-4: 45 p.

MOTTET, M. G. 1980. Research problems concerning the culture of clam spat and seed. Wash. State Dep. Fish. Tech. Rep. 63: 106 p.

QUAYLE, D. B. 1960. The intertidal bivalves of British Columbia. British Columbia Provincial Museum Handbook 17: 104 p.

QUAYLE, D. B., AND N. BOURNE. 1972. The clam fisheries of British Columbia. Bull. Fish. Res. Board Can. 179: 70 p.

SCHINK, T. D., K. A. MCGRAW, AND K. K. CHEW. 1983. Pacific coast clam fisheries. Washington Sea Grant, Univ. of Washington, Washington Sea Grant Tech. Rep. W-83-1: 72 p.

Mussels

BAYNE, B. R. [ED.]. 1976. Marine mussels: their ecology and physiology. Int. Biol. Programme No. 10. Cambridge University Press, Cambridge. 506 p.

CLINE, R., AND D. HAMILL. 1979. Growing oysters and mussels in Maine. Aquaculture Development Workshop, Damariscotta, ME. 46 p.

HERITAGE, G. D. 1983. A blue mussel, *Mytilus edulis* Linnaeus, pilot culture project in south coastal British Columbia. Can. Tech. Rep. Fish. Aquat. Sci. 1174: 27 p.

JENKINS, R. J. 1979. Mussel cultivation in the Marlborough Sounds (New Zealand). New Zealand Fish. Ind. Board, Wellington, New Zealand. 75 p.

KORRINGA, P. 1976. Farming marine organisms low in the food chain: a multi-disciplinary approach to edible seaweed, mussel and clam production. Elsevier Sci. Publ. Co., New York, NY. 264 p.

LUTZ, R. A. [ED.]. 1980. Mussel culture and harvest: a North American perspective. Elsevier Sci. Publ. Co., New York, NY. 350 p.

MAGOON, C., AND R. VINING. 1981. Introduction to shellfish aquaculture in the Puget Sound region. State of Washington, Dep. Nat. Res., Olympia, WA. 68 p.

TILLAPAUGH, D. L., AND J. C. EDWARDS. 1980. A permit and license guide for the prospective aquaculturist. Province of British Columbia, Ministry of Environment, Marine Resources Branch, Victoria, B.C. 23 p.

SKIDMORE, D., AND K. K. CHEW. 1985. Mussel aquaculture in Puget Sound. Washington Sea Grant Tech. Rep. 85-4: 57 p.

Oysters

CHEW, K. K. [ED.]. 1982. Proceedings of the North American oyster workshop. World Mariculture Society, Spec. Publ. 1: 300 p.

KORRINGA, P. 1976. Farming the cupped oysters of the genus *Crassostrea*. Developments in aquaculture and fisheries science, 2. Elsevier Scientific Pub. Co., Amsterdam—Oxford—New York. 224 p.

KORRINGA, P. 1976. Farming the flat oysters of the genus *Ostrea*. Development in aquaculture and fisheries science, 3. Elsevier Scientific Pub. Co., Amsterdam—Oxford—New York. 238 p.

QUAYLE, D. B. 1969. Pacific oyster culture in British Columbia. Bull. Fish. Res. Board Can. 169: 192 p.

QUAYLE, D. B. 1971. Pacific oyster raft culture in British Columbia. Bull. Fish. Res. Board Can. 178: 34 p.

QUAYLE, D. B., AND D. W. SMITH. 1976. A guide to oyster farming. Marine Resources Branch, Dep. Rec. and Travel Industry. Victoria, B.C. 54 p.

VENTILLA, R. F. 1984. Recent developments in the Japanese oyster culture industry. Advances in Marine Biology, Vol. 21 Academic Press, p. 1—57.

YONGE, C. M. 1960. Oysters. Collins, London and Glasgow.

Scallops

BOURNE, N. 1969. Scallop resources of British Columbia. Fish. Res. Board Can. Tech. Rep. 104: 60 p.

MOTTET, M. G. 1979. A review of the fishery biology and culture of scallops. Wash. State Dep. Fish. Tech. Rep. 39: 100 p.

VENTILLA, R. F. 1982. The scallop industry in Japan. Advances in Marine Biology, Vol. 20 Academic Press, p. 309—382.

Paralytic shellfish poisoning

WHITE, A. W. 1983. Red tides. Underwater World Factsheet, Communications Directorate, Dep. Fish. Oceans, Ottawa, Ont. 6 p.

QUAYLE, D. B. 1966. Paralytic shellfish poisoning—safe shellfish. Fish. Res. Board Can., Pacific Biological Station, Nanaimo, B.C. 6 p.

QUAYLE, D. B. 1969. Paralytic shellfish poisoning in British Columbia. Bull. Fish. Res. Board Can. 168: 68 p.

Octopus

HARTWICK, E. B. 1983. *Octopus dofleini. In* P. Boyle [ed.] Cephalopod Life Cycles, Vol. 1. Academic Press, London: 277–291.

HARTWICK, E. B., R. F. AMBROSE, AND S. M. C. ROBINSON. 1984. Dynamics of shallow-water populations of *Octopus dofleini*. Mar. Biol. 82: 65–72.

MOTTET, M. G. 1975. The fishing biology of *Octopus dofleini* (Wilker). Wash. Dep. Fish. Tech. Rep. 16: 39 p.

ROBINSON, S. M. C. 1983. Growth of the giant Pacific octopus *Octopus dofleini martini* on the west coast of British Columbia. M.Sc. thesis, University of British Columbia, Vancouver, B.C.

ROPER, C. F. E., M. J. SWEENEY, AND C. E. NAVEN. 1984. FAO species catalogue. Vol. 3. Cephlopods of the world. An annotated and illustrated catalogue of species of interest to fisheries. FAO Fish. Synop. (125) Vol. 3: 277 p.

Squid

BERNARD, F. R. 1980. Preliminary report on the potential commercial squid of British Columbia. Can. Tech. Rep. Fish. Aquat. Sci. 942: 51 p.

BERNARD, F. R. 1981. Canadian west coast flying squid experimental fishery. Can. Ind. Rep. Fish. Aquat. Sci. 122: 23 p.

FIELDS, W. G. 1965. The structure, development, food relations, and life history of the squid, *Loligo opalescens* BERRY. Calif. Dep. Fish Game 36(4): 366–377.

RECHSIEK, C. W., AND H. W. FREY [ED.]. 1978. Biological, oceanographic and acoustic aspects of the market squid, *Loligo opalscens* BERRY. Calif. Dep. Fish Game 169: 185 p.

ROBINSON, S. M. C., AND G. S. JAMIESON. 1984. Report on Canadian commercial fishery for flying squid using drifting gill nets off the coast of British Columbia. Can. Ind. Rep. Fish. Aquat. Sci. 150: 25 p.

ROPER, C. F. E., M. J. SWEENEY, AND C. E. NAVEN. 1984. FAO species catalogue. Vol. 3. Cephalopods of the world. An annotated and illustrated catalogue of species of interest to fisheries. FAO Fish. Synop. (125) Vol. 3: 277 p.

SLOAN, N. A. 1984. Canadian–Japanese experimental fishery for oceanic squid off British Columbia, summer 1983. Can. Ind. Rep. Fish. Aquat. Sci. 152: 42 p.

Crab

BUTLER, T. H. 1960. Maturity and breeding of the Pacific edible crab, *Cancer magister* Dana. J. Fish. Res. Board Can. 17(5): 641–646.

BUTLER, T. H. 1961. Growth and age determination of the Pacific crab, *Cancer magister* Dana. J. Fish. Res. Board Can. 18(5): 873–891.

HART, J. F. L. 1982. Crabs and their relatives. British Columbia Provincial Museum Handbook 40: 267 p.

JAMIESON, G. S. 1985. The Dungeness crab (*Cancer magister*) fisheries of British Columbia. Proc. Symp. Dungeness crab biology and management. Lowell Wakefield Fish. Symp. Ser., Anchorage, Alaska. Alaska Sea Grant Rep. 85-3: 37–60.

JAMIESON, G. S., AND N. A. SLOAN. 1985. King crabs in British Columbia. Proc. International King Crab Symposium. Lowell Wakefield Fish. Symp. Ser. Anchorage, Alaska, Alaska Sea. Grant Rep. 85-12: 49–62.

SLOAN, N. A. 1985. Life history characteristics of fjord-dwelling golden king crabs, *Lithodes aequispina* Benedict, from northern British Columbia, Canada. Mar. Ecol. Prog. Ser. 22: 219–228.

Shrimp

BUTLER, T. H. 1964. Growth, reproduction, and distribution of pandallid shrimps in British Columbia. J. Fish. Res. Board Can. 21: 1403–1452.

BUTLER, T. H. 1970. Synopsis of biological data on the prawn *Pandalus platyceros* Brandt, 1851. FAO Fish. Rep. 57(4): 1289–1315.

BUTLER, T. H. 1980. Shrimps of the Pacific coast of Canada. Can. Bull. Fish. Aquat. Sci. 202: 280 p.

Euphausiids

FULTON, J., AND R. LeBRASSEUR. 1984. Euphausiids of the continental shelf and slope of the Pacific coast of Canada. La mer 22: 268–276.

HEATH, W. A. 1977. The ecology and harvesting of euphausiids in the Strait of Georgia. Ph.D. thesis, University of British Columbia, Vancouver, B.C.

LeBRASSEUR, R. J., AND J. FULTON. 1967. A guide to zooplankton of the northeastern Pacific Ocean. Fish. Res. Board Can. Circ. 84: 34 p.

MACHLINE, J., AND L. R. FISHER. 1969. The biology of euphausiids, p. 1–454. *In* F. S. Russel and M. Young [ed.] Advances in marine biology, Vol. 7. Academic Press Inc., London.

OMORI, M. 1978. Zooplankton fisheries of the world: a review. Mar. Biol. 48: 199–205.

PARSONS, T. R. 1972. Plankton as a food source. Underwater J. 4: 30–37.

Marine Plants

ABBOTT, I. A., AND E. Y. DAWSON. 1978. How to know the seaweeds. Second Ed. Pictured Key Nature Series, Wm. C. Brown Co. Publ., Dubuque, Iowa. 141 p.

WAALAND, J. R. 1977. Common seaweeds of the Pacific coast. Pacific Search Press. 120 p.

SEAGEL, R. F. 1971. Guide to common seaweeds of British Columbia. British Columbia Provincial Museum of Natural History and Anthropology, Dep. Recreat. Conserv., Handbook No. 27: 330 p.

SHIELDS, T. L., G. S. JAMIESON, AND P. E. SPROUT. 1985. Spawn-on-kelp fisheries in the Queen Charlotte Islands and northern British Columbia coast — 1982 and 1983. Can. Tech. Rep. Fish. Aquat. Sci. 1372: 53 p.

Resource Management

BERNARD, F. R. [ED.]. 1975. Assessment of invertebrate stocks off the west coast of Canada (1981). Can. Tech. Rep. Fish. Aquat. Sci. 1974: 39 p.

JAMIESON, G. S. [ED.]. 1984. 1982 Shellfish Management Advice, Pacific Region. Can. MS Rep. Fish. Aquat. Sci. 1774: 71 p.

JAMIESON, G. S. [ED.]. 1985. 1983 and 1984 Shellfish Management Advice, Pacific Region. Can. MS Rep. Fish. Aquat. Sci. 1848: 107 p.

RICKER, W. E. 1975. Computation and interpretation of biological statistics of fish populations. Bull. Fish. Res. Board Can. 191: 382 p.

APPENDIX 1

ECHINODERMS

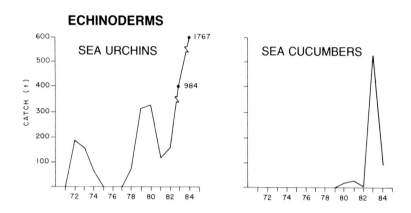

FIG. A. Annual landings of enchinoderms exploited in British Columbia.

MOLLUSCS

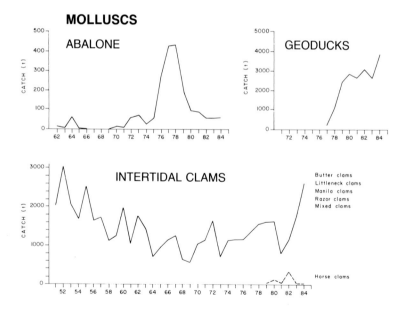

FIG. B. Annual landings of molluscs exploited in British Columbia.

86

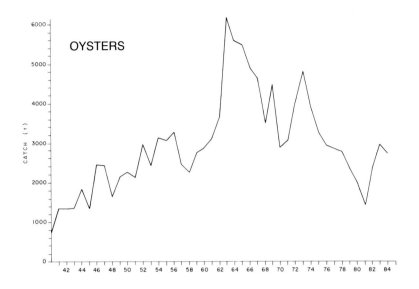

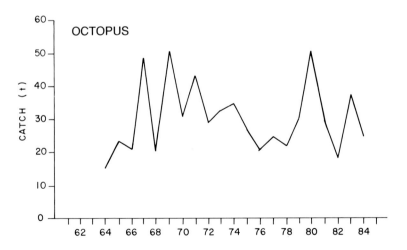

FIG. B. (*Concluded.*)

87

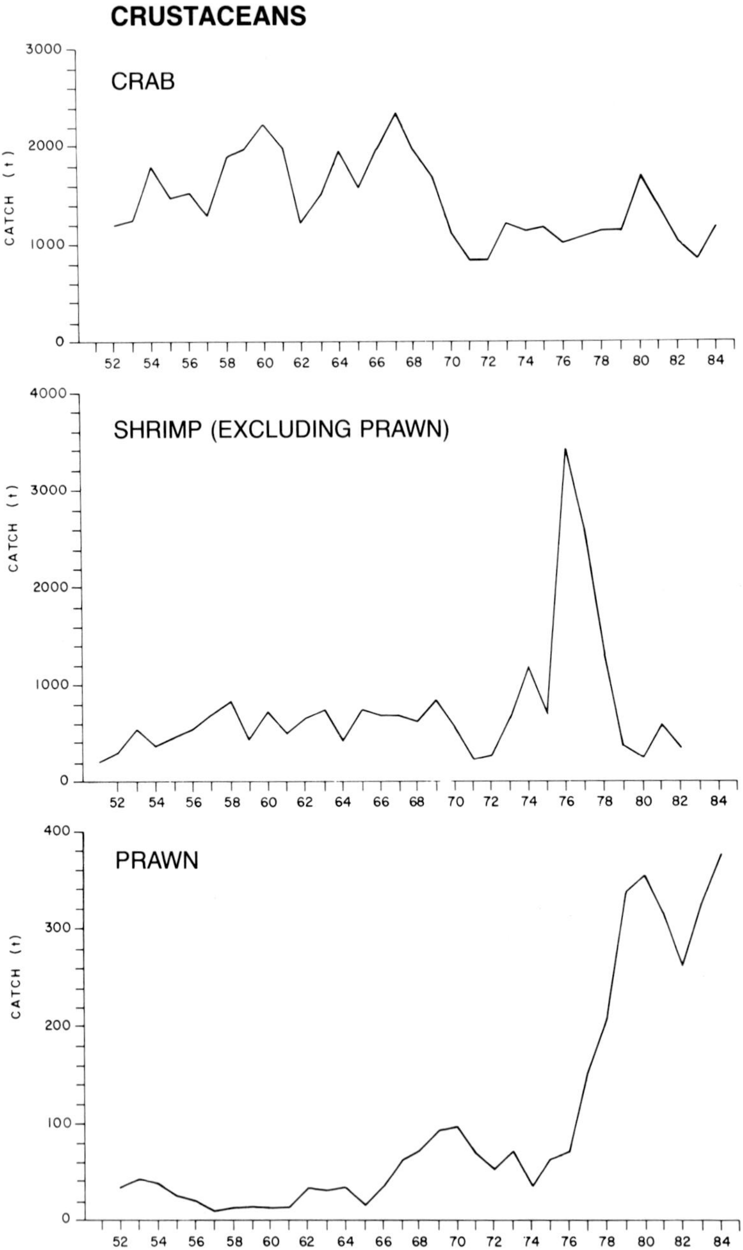

CRUSTACEANS

CRAB

SHRIMP (EXCLUDING PRAWN)

PRAWN

FIG. C. Annual landings of crustaceans exploited in British Columbia.

88

APPENDIX 2

TABLE A. Quantity and value of B.C. fish landings by species — 1984. (Source: Fisheries Production Statistics of British Columbia 1984. Min. Environment, Fisheries Branch, Victoria, B.C.)

	Quantity landed (t)	Landed value ($'000)	Landed price ($/kg)
Salmon	47 865	144 814	$3.03
Herring	33 875	44 365	1.31
Halibut	4 033	9 419	2.34
Groundfish			
Dogfish	2 441	551	0.23
Flounder	169	53	0.31
Hake	33 596	5 213	0.16
Lingcod	3 707	2 183	0.59
Grey cod	3 622	1 765	0.49
Pacific ocean perch	7 043	2 975	0.42
Pollock	596	136	0.23
Rockfish	7 489	3 978	0.53
Sablefish	3 852	6 998	1.82
Skate	390	56	0.14
Sole	3 225	2 072	0.64
Turbot	360	75	0.21
Other groundfish	389	7	0.02
Subtotal	66 879	26 062	
Invertebrates			
Abalone	58	530	9.14
Clams (intertidal)	2 622	2 763	1.05
Crabs	1 155	4 558	3.95
Geoducks	3 483	2 937	0.84
Octopus	25	56	2.24
Oysters	2 897	2 109	0.73
Shrimp and prawns	914	4 284	4.69
Other shellfish	1 892	808	0.43
Subtotal	13 046	18 045	
Other species	135	225	1.67
Total	165 833	242 930